SELECTED WORKS OF PEARL JEPHCOTT: SOCIAL ISSUES AND SOCIAL RESEARCH

Volume 2

SOME YOUNG PEOPLE

SOME YOUNG PEOPLE

PEARL JEPHCOTT

Foreword by
SIR ARTHUR BRYANT

LONDON AND NEW YORK

First published in 1954 by George Allen & Unwin Ltd

This edition first published in 2023
by Routledge
4 Park Square, Milton Park, Abingdon, Oxon OX14 4RN

and by Routledge
605 Third Avenue, New York, NY 10158

Routledge is an imprint of the Taylor & Francis Group, an informa business

© 1954 Pearl Jephcott
© 2023 Josephine Koch

All rights reserved. No part of this book may be reprinted or reproduced or utilised in any form or by any electronic, mechanical, or other means, now known or hereafter invented, including photocopying and recording, or in any information storage or retrieval system, without permission in writing from the publishers.

Trademark notice: Product or corporate names may be trademarks or registered trademarks, and are used only for identification and explanation without intent to infringe.

British Library Cataloguing in Publication Data
A catalogue record for this book is available from the British Library

ISBN: 978-1-032-33020-4 (Set)
ISBN: 978-1-032-33006-8 (Volume 2) (hbk)
ISBN: 978-1-032-33012-9 (Volume 2) (pbk)
ISBN: 978-1-003-31773-9 (Volume 2) (ebk)

DOI: 10.4324/9781003317739

Publisher's Note
The publisher has gone to great lengths to ensure the quality of this reprint but points out that some imperfections in the original copies may be apparent.

Disclaimer
The publisher has made every effort to trace copyright holders and would welcome correspondence from those they have been unable to trace.

New Foreword to the Reissue of *Some Young People*

Pearl Jephcott (1900–1980) spent the early part of her career working in youth clubs and clubs for girls, and as such, the experiences of young people in such clubs offered a rich seam for her early writing and publications. Books such as *Clubs for Girls* (1943), *Girls Growing Up* (1944) and *Rising Twenty: Some Notes on Ordinary Girls* (1948) are Pearl Jephcott's early foray into documenting and exploring the lived realities of everyday lives of mainly working-class young people. The experiences of young people were to form a golden thread which linked all of her main publications and some of these early books, from her MA thesis entitled *'Studies of employed adolescent girls'* onto her later writings on youth, leisure and community. As part of this, in 1954 Pearl writes and compiles *Some Young People*. This was a book that was to become something of a template for her later publications and includes a very detailed 'prefatory note' on the objective aims and approaches used in the research. It's a note which signals an attention to detail that was to become so typical of her writing. Supported by a detailed discussion of research design, readers are given full access to how the research was conducted.

The research outlined in the book was funded by King George's Jubilee Trust with the aim of exploring why a large portion of adolescents do not belong to youth organisations and why so many who do join leave so soon. The research took place from 1950 to 1952 and focused on areas in central London, Nottingham, Oxfordshire and Buckinghamshire. These locations were selected to reflect different 'contexts' for youth clubs. For example, Pearl suggests that the Nottingham district was chosen as it was typical of the city's working-class neighbourhoods whereas Oxfordshire was marked by villages that are apart from each other. London was defined by its metropolitan variety whereas Nottingham was characterised by its uniformity.

The sample comprised of 939 boys and girls aged 14 to 17 who were interviewed about their experiences of youth clubs and uniformed young people's organisations. However, as is typical of much of Pearl's work, Pearl does not only simply focus on the young people themselves but also on the social context including community and family life.

In reading the book it may well feel that some of the debates, references, and concerns are slightly dated and belong to another era. This is possibly correct, but it does not detract from the value of what Pearl Jephcott has produced here. *Some Young People* offers insights into the growing concerns the society had around adolescents and young people. It's written during a time when there is increased anxiety about antisocial behaviour. What Pearl offers here is the antidote by reflecting upon the pro-social behaviour fostered by youth clubs and young peoples uniformed organisations. Pearl Jephcott was a passionate believer in the value of the club for helping young people having witnessed first-hand the benefits the club membership could have in the earlier part of her career.

Beyond the substantive content, in *Some Young People* Pearl uses an approach to data presentation and analysis that will come to typify her analytical lens. This was a preference for allowing respondents to speak for themselves rather than have their experiences presented in aggregated form or lost in numerical data. Rather than translating all of the interview material into simple numerical form, Pearl writes detailed vignettes or short stories about the young people being studied. She uses their words and their stories that they tell about club membership alongside aspects of their everyday lives, from keeping pets to belief in God. Such an approach empowers the young respondents and gives voice to their concerns rather than, as was typical of the time, the older researcher or writer assuming they knew best and presenting their interpretation of what the young people might have said. It's an exercise in autobiographical sociology well before the biographical turn that was to become prominent in the social sciences thirty or so years after this book was written.

From earlier in her career Pearl Jephcott was an innovator. A practice-based sociologist who saw analytical value in aspects of social lives she observed. She honed her craft of observe, record, reflect, repeat in her richly detailed personal diaries. Combining text and image, Pearl's notes reveal a sophisticated sociological imagination. It is her imagination, revealed through her practice that ensures her work continues to resonate.

John Goodwin
University of Leicester
October 2022

SOME YOUNG PEOPLE

A study, sponsored by King George's Jubilee Trust of adolescent boys and girls in three areas, with special reference to their membership of youth groups.

SOME YOUNG PEOPLE

Compiled by
PEARL JEPHCOTT
author of
Girls Growing Up, Rising Twenty

Foreword by Sir Arthur Bryant
C.B.E., LL.D.

GEORGE ALLEN AND UNWIN LTD
RUSKIN HOUSE MUSEUM STREET LONDON

FIRST PUBLISHED IN 1954

This book is copyright under the Berne Convention. Apart from any fair dealing for the purposes of private study, research, criticism or review, as permitted under the Copyright Act 1911, no portion may be reproduced by any process without written permission. Enquiry should be made to the publisher.

*Printed in Great Britain
in 12 point Fournier type
By Simson Shand Limited
London, Hertford and Harlow*

FOREWORD

by

Arthur Bryant

'SOME YOUNG PEOPLE' sounds rather a formidable abstraction. Yet its subject is no abstraction. It concerns what we all were once—boys or girls on the threshold of life faced with life's problems and the necessity of conforming to a society and world already made. We are all in this together, for on what our 'young people' can be made and make themselves depends the future of England. If we feel that we have inherited much from the past, we are under an obligation to transmit it to posterity. We cannot repay our ancestors for what they left us—institutions that taught us all that makes life full, ennobling and worth living. We can only honour our debt by what we leave in turn to posterity. *Some Young People* is our link with England's future.

Its pages unfold a story of immense significance. They have been written as the result of an enquiry instituted by King George's Jubilee Trust to ascertain the causes of wastage from Youth Organizations and to throw light on the problems of attracting to them boys and girls in the changed conditions of today, and of recruiting to their service men and women with the generosity and capacity to lead and inspire youth. They have been based on the day-by-day life of a thousand or so adolescents living in three representative areas—metropolitan, provincial-urban, and rural. Here, in living portraiture almost as vivid in miniature as the figures in Chaucer's *Canterbury Tales* or Dickens's novels, are the boys and girls of modern Britain who will be the citizens of tomorrow. Here are the children of the Welfare State playing in the drab, crowded streets their games of 'Tin Can Lurkey' and 'Slide Box', or chanting the 20th century folk-refrain, 'Willie, Willie Woodbine, Bring me luck, If you don't, I'll tear you up!' 'There's never no time,' one child told an investigator, 'when some isn't not playing in our street.' Here, too, are our young people as, entering industrial employment, they turn from children into adolescents, seeking, as adolescents will, to be older before their time and to sample the pleasures of experience without experience and without guidance. Here is Eileen, aged 17, to whom leisure means spending money and work earning it, who never thinks about religion, having too much else to do, and believes there is a God but never considers the matter unless frightened; town-bred Ted and Sammy who have acquired a passion for birds from reading a Victorian tome of their grandfather's on natural history and who spend all their spare time bicycling to neighbouring woods, fields and ponds to collect data for their naturalist's journal; Harry, aged 17, whose passion is cycle-racing, who likes the girls and has an ear for classical music, and occasionally—most rare feat among his contemporaries—reads a book, and who left the Scouts because 'it was all talk and no do'; Rose, the 'pretty, gentle, pink-and-white creature who should have been a shepherdess but today minds her machines', has three elder and five younger brothers and sisters to whom she acts as mother, and who, in a discreet but diligent way, spends her leisure with a girl friend of like mind at the pictures, at dances and 'up the Street', trying to acquire a boy friend. And here are others who, turned loose from overcrowded homes into noisy, uninspired, undisciplined streets, nourished on popular Sunday newspapers, strip-cartoons, sex-novelettes and the cultural fare of the cheap cinema with its fug, noise and lack of standards, and who, ignorant of Christian lore, morality and discipline, and with all the natural instincts of youth starved or perverted, become the inevitable prey of the gang-leader or, at best, grow up to lead, despite all the material opportunities of our age, inert, stunted and purposeless lives.

The Youth Organizations are doing, and have long done, a great job of work, and King George's Jubilee Trust exists to help them in their noble, selfless mission. But they are touching only about a third of the adolescents in the country, and are having to cope, often with the equipment and sometimes with the ideas of twenty or even fifty years ago, with a revolutionary social situation and a dangerously confused society. And they are desperately short of leaders and workers of the right kind.

The Report inevitably focuses a searchlight on their difficulties and to some extent on their deficiencies. Yet it indicates, with stark but salutary realism, the challenge facing both them and every man and woman who cares for the future of the country, and offers, with that challenge, an illimitable opportunity. Here, in 'the crowded, gardenless houses and the sterile streets' that deny to youth nearly all the things that are necessary for constructive leisure, is a new, underdeveloped and scarcely explored world that a generation of new Elizabethans with vision, courage and a sense of adventure might transform into a society worthy of England's past greatness. New ideas are needed, new ways of awakening the dormant energies, idealism and faith of the protected yet at present drifting youth of the Welfare State, new organizations with techniques and approach in keeping with the fashions of an age which prides itself above everything else on being 'modern' and up-to-date. Yet what are needed above all are not better organizations and organization, but men and women with the greatness of heart and courage to go out with both hands open to help the young by contact, friendship and example. For those willing to do so the greatest of all opportunities is waiting, and the greatest of all rewards. To them from the overburdened Youth Organizations goes up the age-long cry that the fields are white with harvest and the reapers are few: 'Come over into Macedonia and help us!'

PREFATORY NOTE

THE OBJECT OF THE ENQUIRY	To see why a larger proportion of adolescents do not belong to youth organizations and why so many who do join soon leave.
SPONSORED BY	King George's Jubilee Trust under the direction of their Standing Research and Advisory Committee.
COMMITTEE APPOINTED TO CARRY OUT THE ENQUIRY	
Chairman	Major-General J. F. Hare, C.B., D.S.O., Research Secretary, King George's Jubilee Trust.
University Members	L. J. Barnes, Esq., M.C., M.A., University of Oxford. G. B. Jeffery, Esq., M.A., D.SC., F.R.S., University of London. Professor W. O. Lester-Smith, C.B.E., M.A., LL.D., University of London. Professor E. A. Peel, M.A., PH.D., University of Birmingham. Professor A. Radford, B.SC.(ECON.), University of Nottingham.
Research Staff	Miss Pearl Jephcott, M.A. Miss Monica W. Le Mare. E. F. Piercy, Esq., O.B.E., PH.D.
DATE	1950–52.
PLACE	Small areas in Central London, Nottingham, Oxfordshire and Bucks.
PEOPLE	939 boys and girls aged 14–17 inclusive.
NAMES	These are fictitious when referring to persons and places in the areas concerned.
AREA REPORTS	This report is a compilation of the fuller reports of the three research workers which include statistics relating to the joining and leaving of organizations.

For permission to consult the full reports application should be made to King George's Jubilee Trust, 166 Piccadilly, London, W.1.

In Appendix III, on page 167, acknowledgment is made of the help which was given during the Enquiry by many organizations and individuals. It remains for us to say here that we are deeply indebted to the members of the Special Committee which directed the Enquiry, both the University members who gave so much of their time and the three research workers, Dr Piercy, Miss Jephcott and Miss Le Mare, on whom fell the main burden of the work. We are especially grateful to Miss Jephcott, who undertook the difficult task of co-ordinating the three area reports and writing the final report.

(*signed*) **T. N. F. WILSON**
Secretary
King George's Jubilee Trust
on behalf of the Administrative Council

CONTENTS

Foreword by Sir Arthur Bryant	PAGE 5
Prefatory Note	9
PART I: THE OBJECT OF THE ENQUIRY	13
How the Enquiry was conducted	
PART II: PLACE AND PEOPLE (TOWN AREAS)	
London	24
Nottingham	29
The boys and girls	35
Passing the time	54
PART III: RELATIONSHIP WITH YOUTH ORGANIZATIONS IN TOWN AREAS	
Who joined what?	69
What appeared to affect joining	70
Personality and Family	73
Education	77
Employment	81
'My Friends'	87
Nature of the youth organizations in Nottingham	90
PART IV: THE ENQUIRY IN THE COUNTRY AREAS (OXFORDSHIRE AND BUCKS)	96
PART V: CONCLUSIONS	
The boys and girls	104
The youth organizations	117
The Service of Youth	136
A Summing up	139
APPENDICES	
Appendix I—Terms of Reference	157
Appendix II—	160
Table 1. Number interviewed; age; at school or at work; education; whether member of a youth organization at time of interview	
Diagram	

SOME YOUNG PEOPLE

PAGE

Table 2. Numbers belonging to a youth organization or evening class at time of interview:
(London and Nottingham)

Table 3. Numbers belonging to a youth organization or evening class at time of interview:
(Oxfordshire and Bucks)

Table 4. Membership and attendance at youth organizations (Nottingham)

Table 5A. Seven days' record: (Nottingham)

5B. Cinema attendance (London and Nottingham)

5C. Sample wages (Nottingham)

Appendix III—Acknowledgments 167

PART I

THE OBJECT OF THE ENQUIRY

BOYS AND GIRLS of teen-age are curious creatures. Any parent will affirm this on occasion, and will add that one of the adolescent's less predictable features is the company which he chooses to keep. It is not only fathers and mothers who trace the course of their children's friendships with alarm or satisfaction. Employers and teachers, the parson and the probation officer, welcome the youngster who selects his companions with circumspection.

One aspect of these early friendships is full of riddles. Why do some boys and girls spend most of their free time with a small, tightly knit set of friends, while others prefer a formal organization and still others confine themselves to 'just me and my mate'? Or again, why does a youngster who has been an enthusiastic member of a youth group for several years suddenly lose interest in it? If so many adolescents place high value on their Church Fellowships, their Cadets, their Girl Guides and so on, why do others of much the same ability and upbringing either sample and disregard these organizations or maybe never give the notion of joining a thought? If any explanation of these divergent outlooks could be disentangled it might clarify the principles which should govern the provision for adolescents' leisure. It might also produce some much needed information on the grouping propensities of adolescents and on the changing habits of young workers in a Welfare State. It might even illuminate the problem of how to re-whet the appetite of those who have been fed the educational cake for ten long years. Results of more immediate use might also be forthcoming, such as suggestions for increasing the adolescent membership of societies and hypotheses suitable for an organization to test for itself.

It was to investigate such questions as these, and in particular the reaction of those aged fourteen to seventeen to their local youth organizations, that King George's Jubilee Trust undertook the Enquiry from which this book has arisen.* By the terms of the Trust Deed its funds must be used for the welfare of young people. It is therefore keenly interested in what impact the youth organizations appear to be making. That they produce no impression on a large number of adolescents is well known. Surveys suggest that about two in three adolescents refuses to take advantage of these organizations which, it must be remembered, are specifically set up for young people, are a part of the official Education service and are aided by public money. 'Refuse' is a strong word. It has been used advisedly here to emphasize what is an essential character of the youth organization, viz. that the youngster joins of his own free choice. Whether it is a good thing for him to belong or not is another question. Some would argue that to-day's adolescent is already over-directed and that he should be left severely alone in his free time to solve his own problems in his own way. Others believe that, at adolescence, most children from most types of home benefit from the experience which voluntary membership of an organized group provides.

The whole subject bristles with difficulties. Whatever the truth of the matter, those responsible for this particular study were required to hold neutral views. They were knowledgeable about youth groups certainly, but held no brief for them. They were agreed however that it would be useful to find out what certain boys and girls really thought of the organizations in their own neighbourhood. With this in mind they made contact during the course of two years with about nine hundred boys and girls aged fourteen, fifteen, sixteen and seventeen. These youngsters' opinions and actions were the first matters that the Enquirers tackled. They supplemented and clarified the boys' and girls' own viewpoints by consulting many of the adults who were meeting these particular adolescents in their daily round of home and school, work and play.

*See p. 157—Terms of Reference.

THE OBJECT OF THE ENQUIRY

The Enquiry was concerned with ordinary boys and girls, and faced the normal scatter of good and bad, boorish and bookish. The idle apprentice was there but so was the potential leader. The scatter-brain too was present, cheerfully ready to give his snap answer to the most searching of questions. The adolescents, of course, were not the only ones with quirks and quiddities; and during the two years the boys and girls doubtless hauled some odd fish into their own nets. But on the whole the relationship between enquirers and adolescents was a good one.

Although the former set out to discuss just one feature in the life of the youngsters, viz. their relationship with the local youth groups, every note the enquirers wrote down about a boy or girl was informed by the necessity to make even the briefest sentence reveal something of his whole person. In many cases even brief contact with a boy forced the older man to feel a concern for the younger one, in the Quaker sense. Indeed it was noticeable during the two years of the Enquiry how much its emphasis did shift from the youth group on to the boys and girls themselves. The findings, too, though originally intended for those busy with the technicalities of youth work, tended to be presented also to the ordinary citizen. In general the latter regards the adolescent world as of no particular concern to him except at such times as he is disturbed by reports of vicious assaults perpetrated by youths in their teens. The great majority of the boys and girls encountered were of course 'good' youngsters, and were never remotely involved with the police, but all were beginning to mould themselves according to the pressures of the adult world and certain of these pressures were definitely unfavourable.

A final point, and one which those responsible for the Enquiry noted again and again, was how frequently a youngster responded to and throve on the interest of some older person. This was so marked that those who produced this Report felt that it would be valueless should it merely lead to more organizations for adolescents without warming some older hearts towards actual living boys and actual living girls.

HOW THE ENQUIRY WAS CONDUCTED

IT WAS planned that the Enquiry as to why boys and girls do or do not join a youth group should be completed in two years; that a Pilot Enquiry should be undertaken in several small areas to determine the character and location of the main ones and that a factual schedule should be filled in for every boy and girl aged fourteen to seventeen living in the areas. The schedule, however, was to be no more than a supplement to information collected from other sources. The Pilot areas selected were in London, Nottingham and Oxfordshire, and were chosen with certain points in mind. The London area was to provide experience of problems connected with adolescents and their organizations which were typical of Central London. The Nottingham area was to be representative of the city's more stable and prosperous working-class districts. And that in Oxfordshire was to include several dissimilar villages which were definitely rural and had neither the characteristics nor amenities of a small town.

In London a part of the Borough of 'Northbury' (see p. 24) was chosen for the Pilot Enquiry. A list of those aged fourteen to seventeen living in the selected area was drawn up from information supplied by the Youth Employment Officer and the Education Officer of the London County Council. This list was not complete as it omitted the children attending Grammar Schools, as well as any newcomers to the area. But the former omission was rectified and the final list, though by no means comprehensive, was thought to be a fair cross section of Northbury's adolescent population. Anyone familiar with the habits of the boys and girls of Central London will realize that in the time available, and with voluntary part-time helpers, it was a formidable task to conduct careful interviews with about three hundred youngsters. However a group of men and women, each of whom had a good deal of experience of adolescents and youth organizations, divided the area between them. These helpers were not only responsible for interviewing but were asked to make a small sociological survey of the immediate vicinity of the homes of the boys and girls they met. They were also asked to consult parents, teachers, officials and business men, and were invited to draw up a list of recommendations that would apply to the Enquiry's problem as seen in that particular part of Northbury.

In Nottingham the district known as 'Robin Wood' (see p. 29) was chosen as typical of those areas in which much of the city's working class population now lives and is likely to live for many years. Within Robin Wood a single polling district (with a circumference of about a mile) was selected for the Enquiry, and here an introduction was obtained to a Trade Union official who had two adolescent sons. With help from this family, and by a process of snowballing and determined door knocking, a register of about 135 names—all those aged fourteen, fifteen, sixteen and seventeen living in the selected polling district—was drawn up. The Nottingham group of interviewers planned to make themselves known to these boys and girls before they made any contact with official bodies. Local press publicity was avoided, but the Enquiry's national character was stressed, and a large-scale plan of the locality, demonstrating that Robin Wood had been chosen, proved a useful bit of ammunition. A small confined area like Robin Wood spills many of its inhabitants into the streets, particularly in summer. In the process of building up the register, interviewing the more amenable boys and girls and frequenting the local cinemas, cafés and evening classes, contact was established with other members of the adolescents' families, and especially with their younger brothers and sisters. Immediately after the interviewers had set up some kind of relationship with the last of the adolescent boys and girls, they began to get in touch with the schools, Churches, youth organizations and any societies to which the adolescents belonged. The chief omission was the boys' and girls' employers, but the interviewers did not, as yet, feel themselves on good enough terms with many of the youngsters to suggest meeting these. It was a laborious business to see all the boys and girls from scratch, so to speak, but it ensured what was felt to be of first importance, viz. that the adolescents and their families should feel that the interviewers had absolutely no axe to grind for youth organizations.

In Oxfordshire the first village to be visited was 'Melbury' (see p. 96). Here a list of those aged fourteen to seventeen was drawn up from old school registers; and the boys and girls were approached direct. They all turned up at the first meeting, and filled in the schedule. At 'Chadlicott,' the second village, it was planned to meet the adolescents through the local Girl Guides and Boys' Brigade. Eighteen of the village's twenty-eight adolescents came to the first meeting. A letter was sent to those who had made no response and homes were visited. At this meeting a talk was given on the Enquiry, and the boys and girls were told the part they could play in it. They were then divided into small groups, each with an interviewer, and started on the schedule at whatever point came easiest to them. The effort required to write the answers to a printed set of questions helped to keep them interested and to forget themselves, although it normally took up to a couple of hours to complete the form. Interviews in the home were more difficult. It generally meant that the interviewer had to fill in the schedule himself.

In all three areas the Enquiry aroused a variety of reactions. The schedule was invariably too long. Before it was completed the youngster wanted to be off, and the interviewer was exhausted. Another trial was the crowded nature of so many of the rooms in which the interview had to take place. This meant that the important point, the youngster's own views, was liable to be shouted down. Or there was the home where the interviewer could hardly get any conversation going. Some parents were very helpful; but others gave no sort of encouragement themselves nor did they urge their youngsters to try to be co-operative or even to keep appointments. There was, of course, no reason why the boys and girls should have taken part in the Enquiry, but having said they would it seemed reasonable to expect them to keep their word. The exact purpose of the Enquiry was not easy to put into plain words. In Nottingham many of the boys and girls never did realize its implications, nor were they much interested in its purpose even when they were so agreeable as to provide information. Certain of the boys were scared that it might be a back-handed attempt to hustle them into an organization, though any hint that it might lead to more playing fields at once gave it importance. A good many of the older girls were inclined to jib at the whole thing. It seemed to them, as indeed it was, an intrusion into their private lives.

As far as accuracy went in all three areas the boys and girls were remarkably frank, nor did they lay claim to interests they did not possess. The enquirers were doubtless foxed sometimes—what interviewer is not?—but on the whole the facts given appeared to be reasonably accurate when checked by outside sources. In Nottingham, too, it was noted that boys and girls held to their reasons why they had left an organization quite consistently, and sometimes repeated in almost identical words what they had said on the subject some months earlier. One danger that did arise was that more material was forthcoming from the Grammar than the ex-Secondary Modern School youngster. The former could both fill in the schedule for himself (which extended the time for talk) and he could marshal his thoughts better. It was the less literate youngster, from the home that was poor in every sense, who tended to give the scrappy doorstep interview—just the one, so often, who had little use for any youth organization. It is, moreover, always necessary to bear in mind that a sociological enquiry of this kind tends to attract the unusual rather than the normal individual. The latter is too busy with his own affairs to bother seriously about something that he only half comprehends. Despite all this, the interviewers worked in the belief that by studying the youngsters hard enough and long enough in their environment, and by making as little disturbance of existing patterns as possible, the significant factors that affected the Enquiry's main problem would eventually emerge.

To sum up. The chief difference of method in the three areas was that larger numbers and a wider physical world were involved in the London work than in that of Nottingham or Oxfordshire. Not only was the scale far bigger than that of Nottingham or the villages (which made it possible for London to undertake certain statistical analyses) but the population it had to interview was relatively hard-bitten about surveys and door-knocking officials. Its findings, however, were based on information obtained by people who had a first-hand, if not an intensive, knowledge of the situation. In Nottingham the area was so small and homogeneous that it was possible to make a study of certain boys and girls for as long as half their years between fourteen and seventeen, i.e. half the age span with which the Enquiry was concerned. The Oxfordshire villages were far apart from each other and this involved much travel. But there was one great compensation, viz. that it could draw on the detailed information that a rural community possesses about its own members. This enabled a detailed analysis to be made of the reasons for leaving an organization. There is a further point that should be mentioned here. If the Nottingham viewpoint appears to be overstressed in the Report, the explanation is two-fold. In the first place the compiler of the final report had been the senior research worker on the Nottingham Enquiry, and secondly the Nottingham workers were in contact with the same area for two years. London and Oxford had a break both in area and time which allowed them no more than one year's work in each of their areas.

The points which arose out of the Pilot Enquiry were not so much direct answers to the main problem—why adolescents do or do not join a youth organization—as subjects which bore sufficiently on this problem to demand further investigation. To take a few examples. All the areas found that the great majority of the adolescents they talked with had belonged to an organization at some stage. The Oxfordshire interviewers observed that the majority gave up their societies when they left school; and London that the greatest amount of leaving among those of adolescent age occurred during the first twelve months of membership. Nottingham noted that effective membership was higher with those aged fourteen and fifteen than among those of sixteen and seventeen; and that a considerable proportion of the older boys and girls regarded youth organizations as altogether too juvenile for them London and Nottingham found that those who, as adolescents, kept out of societies tended to be below average on a variety of counts. They were of less than normal intelligence, or they were in unsatisfactory jobs, or they came from homes that were in bad repute with the neighbours. In the case of the Nottingham adolescents, and of the girls in particular, social ill-ease appeared to be a major reason for not joining an organization. In view of this alleged shyness ('don't like a crowd', 'no one to go with') it was felt that the significance of the adolescents' special set of friends would repay study. Another thing which the Pilot Enquiry suggested was that the leaving of organizations, and the lack of sufficient interest even to sample them, was sometimes due to the youngster's inability to distinguish what kind of group was most likely to suit his own tastes. It was pointed out by the London Team that each youth unit had a pattern peculiar to itself, and that those who failed to conform to the pattern left. In Oxfordshire, although it was found that the status of the family in the local community seemed to influence the grouping propensities of its adolescent members, no connection was discovered between membership of formal groups and the youngster's general intelligence. In the villages, too, many of the boys and girls pursued in their own self-constituted groups traditional rural entertainments, such as cricket, bathing, etc. In spite of this, however, the Oxford interviewers considered that there was a definite need for more opportunities for organized activities. They also suspected that there was a certain amount of hostility between the adolescent and the adult population. A point on which Oxfordshire and Nottingham agreed was that the adolescent from a normal home in a stable neighbourhood has a supply of ready-made company at hand, in the shape of relatives and of neighbours with whom his parents have a long-standing acquaintance.

The experience obtained from the Pilot Enquiry determined the plan of the main one which was as follows. In London it was thought that if the Pilot method was merely repeated in another area it would be unlikely to produce any substantially different results. Rather than a new geographical area, therefore, the past and present adolescent population of two schools was selected for study. The schools in question were situated in 'Camdington', a neighbouring borough to Northbury. One was a Mixed Secondary Modern School and the other a Technical cum Secondary Modern School (though the interviewers concerned themselves with the latter side only). Those boys and girls of fourteen and fifteen who were still at school were interviewed in school hours, while those of fifteen, sixteen and seventeen who had left school were called upon in their homes. As in the Pilot Enquiry, the interview was supplemented by information from other sources; and any society which attracted a substantial number of the local boys and girls was visited. The greater part of the field work was carried out by a team of voluntary workers from the University of London Extension Association (Westminster College of Commerce Branch). Their energy and persistence merits the highest praise. The Enquiry is particularly indebted to the work of the two leaders, Miss K. Colegate and Miss P. Roden.

In Nottingham the Pilot Enquiry had suggested that the whole business of leaving was often tied up with emotional disturbances—matters which the youngsters would not talk of readily to a stranger. Their brief bald answers to the schedule provided facts of the 'yes-no' variety, but they did not illuminate any subtleties of behaviour. The Pilot Enquiry had also indicated that the youngster's set of particular friends appeared to influence the nature of his attitude to more formal groups. This again was an aspect of the adolescent's life which demanded time to disentangle. It was therefore agreed that Nottingham should carry on its Main Enquiry with the same set of boys and girls as it had met in the Pilot, i.e. the total 14–17 population of the chosen area. The chief difference between the methods adopted in the Pilot and the Main Enquiry was that in the latter more information was sought from official sources. Most of the agencies which were touching or had ever directly affected the adolescent were consulted. They included the Health Service, the Probation Service, various branches of the Educational Service, and especially, of course, the Youth Service. Most of the boys' and girls' employers were met, and their present and former schools, the local Churches, adult organizations, sports clubs and cinemas were visited. Certain shopkeepers and the proprietor of a milk bar were particularly helpful. Contact was also made with practically every youth organization that, according to the youngsters, they had belonged to even if only for a brief period. All told, however, it was with the boys and girls themselves and with their homes that the interviewers spent the bulk of their time.

In Oxfordshire the Main Enquiry started afresh, except that 'Mersham', one of the Pilot villages where only preliminary investigations had been made, was included in the second set of villages to be investigated, together with another village, 'Upper Hinton', which was in Buckinghamshire. It was decided that all subjective information about the adolescents should be collected by one person only, the senior research worker. In both villages most of the boys and girls who were still at school were seen during school hours; and those who had left were invited to meet the research worker in the evening either at the school or, in the case of Upper Hinton, at the youth club. Non-club members were interviewed in their home, though this generally meant that information had to be taken down somewhat hurriedly at the time, or recorded later. A retired teacher from the school and some of the adults in the village helped greatly over these first contacts with the boys and girls. The hundred and thirty-two adolescents interviewed from the two villages had attended a considerable number of schools. Most of these were visited and the youngsters' answers to the schedule were checked. For the Upper Hinton children the Chief Education Officer for Buckinghamshire provided information on their I.Q.s (under three grades). In a similar way, past and present membership of youth organizations was checked with the youth leaders; and general information about adult societies was collected from the latters' officials and members. When possible the information about employment that the schedule had elicited was checked with the firm concerned. In Upper Hinton a final source of information was supplied by the adolescents themselves. They undertook a small survey of the village, examining its physical character, land usage, population, employment and social amenities.

PART II

PLACE AND PEOPLE

LONDON (NORTHBURY AND CAMDINGTON)*

THE LONDON Enquiry took place, as has been indicated, in two somewhat similar districts of Central London, each of which is about two miles as the crow flies from Piccadilly Circus. The hubs of these two districts are themselves a mile and a half apart, although their eastern and western corners are contiguous. 'Central London' suggests the West End, but Northbury and Camdington are ecologically a great distance from Whitehall or Regent Street.

Northbury, the first district, has a long history. In the Middle Ages it lay outside the City wall. After the Great Fire homeless families put up shacks in Northbury's fields, while from the eighteenth century onwards it provided suburban pleasures in the shape of theatres and bathing pools, and met more mundane needs with prisons, pest houses and asylums. It was near enough to the City to be industrialized early, and by the 1930's it was reckoned

* General Information	Borough of 'Northbury' 1950	Borough of 'Camdington' 1950
Population	58,000 (on voting list)	141,300
Enquiry Area	Major part of 3 wards	Past and present population (14–17 years) of two Secondary Mod. Schools.
Enquiry Area population aged 14-17 interviewed	222	421
L.C.C. Register of Recognised Youth Units	64	No information

to contain some of the blackest spots on the poverty map. Many of the parents of the boys and girls whom the interviewers met had lived for years under acute financial strain. They had only been relatively free from insecurity within the last decade. In 1950, however, little genuine poverty was in evidence. Where it did occur it was among old people, with families who had several young children, or with a mother whose husband was dead or ill or had gone off.

Northbury is a drab looking place. The narrow streets of decayed working class houses are tucked behind the main thoroughfares which themselves are flanked by gaunt warehouses and Victorian factories. During the War the whole district was heavily blitzed and it is still riddled with vacant lots and with gaping, shored-up houses. The population is mainly artisan, though a few professional people inhabit one little patch. There is a considerable Italian element. Work is manual and local, within a twopenny bus ride. The men are chiefly in labouring jobs, and the women are employed in tailoring firms and in the Northbury shops. Young married women stay on in their jobs until the arrival of the second baby. Not many of the adolescents' mothers are in full-time work. They do a certain amount of early morning office cleaning, and they often have grandchildren to mind.

Northbury's external appearance certainly does not commend it, nor does a close-up. The majority of the houses are in decayed terraces, two or three stories high, and occupied by several families. Indeed the interviewers only encountered one youngster who had a complete house for his home. The 'buildings', as distinct from the terrace houses, are mostly early and utilitarian tenements, surrounded by an asphalt yard. The flats within them, small, four-roomed affairs, may have as many as seven or eight occupants. A certain number of the boys and girls live in post-war flats. These are admirable homes compared with those of the buildings, though the poorer or more feckless families find their rent too high.

The social life of the borough centres around its markets, its pubs, its back-street shops, its fish frys and a few other traditional meeting places. At the time of the Enquiry, the youngsters did not appear to frequent pubs (they were under age anyhow); but Mum would pop in with a friend and Dad would go round most nights for an hour or so. The family rarely went together. Northbury has little drunkenness; and, according to the police, most of the drinking is done at home. The police also say that prostitution is rare, except among the deserted wives of foreign servicemen. These girls take in 'lodgers' and supplement their income on the streets. They often have children to keep and they have to pay a fairly high rent for their rooms.

The local cinemas provide the bulk of the borough's regular entertainment, though some of the youngsters preferred the more modern houses on the fringe of the West End. A Music-Hall is popular and the Town Hall dances are reasonably well patronized. Several institutions of national repute are situated in Northbury; but the natives firmly disregard them. Nor do the Churches come much into the picture. Few Northbury adults are regular worshippers and the religious bodies are not one of the obviously significant features of the borough's social life.

This portrait is much that of any other of London's sadly-looking though still active relics of nineteenth century industrialism. But the enquirers noted that it had distinctive features. In the first place a great many of the families met had always lived in the borough and few people contemplated leaving it on marriage. Their loyalty was probably an enforced rather than a real one and was caused by the exigencies of the housing shortage. But the Northbury people certainly did spend most of their time locally, and hardly moved beyond places within hailing distance of each other. They travelled neither for work nor pleasures. This attachment was less to the borough than to the immediate vicinity, the block or street in which they lived. Two or three generations of the family had often been born within these small confines and those who married an outsider rather liked to transplant him, if they could, into the family plot. Loyalty to Northbury did however find some focus in the Council. Many councillors had been born in the borough and had lived and worked all their lives there.

They were vigorous about its business; and not least where this concerned the younger citizens.

A second unusual characteristic of the area is its transient, day-time population. Thousands pour through Northbury on their morning journey to the City or to the main line stations. Thousands who come into the borough to work, hurry out of it again at 5.30 p.m. Northbury's industries are not its own nor are they staffed chiefly by local people. Although most of the latter work in or near Northbury, they only comprise a fraction of the total number employed there. Even the school children are not home-grown. The two Grammar schools draw perhaps five per cent of their scholars from the borough, while the rest come from all over London. The Secondary Modern Schools likewise teach a great many pupils from the adjoining boroughs. This local-centred life of the inhabitants and the influx of so large a day-time population make Northbury a strangely isolated place. Indeed the blocks of flats, with their rigidly self-contained life, give it something of the character of a scatter of villages. But it lacks the social assets of a rural community. Northbury has no need to create its amusements nor to support its churches nor to cast a critical eye on its schools. These facilities and services rain from above; and Northbury is more often the passive recipient than the active participator.

Camdington was the second district of Central London with which the Enquiry was concerned. As has been said before, a school and not a geographical population was involved in the Camdington Survey; but most of the boys and girls of the two schools contacted lived within three-quarters of a mile of them and in an area which was roughly two miles long by a third of a mile across. Camdington is a less venerable neighbourhood than Northbury. Long after the latter had been built up, citizens could still walk in the fields of Camdington 'near London'. When the inevitable development did come, at about the time of the Napoleonic Wars, the new streets and crescents (those in which the boys and girls were living) were decent, and urbane. Other, less pleasing building followed. This included the termini of three main-line railway stations and many warehouses and factories. The last major change was the blitz, so severe in this part of London that by 1941 the population of the borough was half of what it had been before the war began.

It is a more drab-looking district than Northbury. This is not only due to the war-time damage, for the houses were frowsty with age and grime before explosion and fire occurred. As in Northbury many of the boys and girls interviewed were living in dreary 'buildings' and many more in tenement houses which, if not technically over-crowded, were very short of space, had no bath, and only a sink-plus-tap and a W.C. which were shared by several families. Most of these houses contained a basement flat which was never really light and was perpetually gritty from the dust that blew straight in from the pavement if a window was open. There was excuse for the squalor of certain of the youngsters' homes.

Although Camdington is a highly industrialized district it has few large factories. But there is a welter of smaller businesses, back-yard affairs whose working conditions are often poor. The main employment is railway work, engineering, building and, of course, the retail trades. A good deal of 'out' work in dressmaking, upholstery, brasswork and toy and flower making is undertaken in the home. As in Northbury not much primary poverty was encountered by the interviewers. Some homes indeed looked quietly prosperous, but it should be remembered that families which contain an adolescent probably have at least one child who is old enough to work. The local people agreed that it was steady employment rather than high wages which had reduced the financial anxiety which was a normal feature of Camdington life before the War. Its recreational facilities, too, are those of Northbury except that the West End cinemas, dance halls and amusement arcades are rather nearer. Camdington has one great asset which Northbury lacks—open spaces. Two parks lie not more than ten minutes' walk from most of the boys' and girls' homes and within a threepenny bus ride there are 300 acres of open land in one of London's great commons.

PLACE AND PEOPLE 29

The enquirers noted that the Camdington population was a more mixed and also a more shifting one than that of Northbury. It showed less evidence of street loyalties. An unusually high proportion of foreigners were encountered, especially Italians, Negroes and Cypriots; and there were many Irish families. The railway termini, too, brought in the temporary visitor together with the problems that he produces, high-priced and odoriferous cafés, pubs with few familiar faces, dubious lodgings and so on. The enquirers did not find the district quite the Gehenna that the *Camdington Herald* (devoted almost entirely to court cases and cinema write-ups) would lead the stranger to suppose. But it certainly had its unsavoury patches where people made no bones about the fly-by-night disappearances and personal disgraces that Northbury would have tried to hush up 'because of what the neighbours will say'. On the other hand, the Camdington people looked smarter and were rather less insular than those in Northbury. This did not mean that they were any more ready to answer the door to a stranger. Indeed they were less friendly than in Northbury and much more inclined to be suspicious of the interviewers.

NOTTINGHAM (ROBIN WOOD)*

The thing that first struck the enquirers about the Nottingham as compared with the London area was the variety of the metropolitan scene and the uniformity of the provincial one. The architecture of the former, the goods it makes, the names on the shops and the notices on the walls reflect a more heterogeneous and stimulating life than that of Robin Wood.

* General Information	District of 'Robin Wood'
Population (estimated)	13,000
Enquiry Area (Pilot and Main Enquiry)	1 polling district of 1 ward within Robin Wood
Enquiry Area population aged 14–17 (approx.)	135
Enquiry Area population aged 14-17 interviewed	**129**

Moreover the latter, for all its byelaw streets, has an odd breath of the country that is woefully absent in Camdington and Northbury. Despite Nottingham's twenty-five square miles and 300,000 people, the Greenwood Tree is never far from Robin Wood. Nottingham itself, although it was chosen for the Enquiry as a typical industrial city, is notably a clean and green one. It is a prosperous city too, for its textiles, bicycles, medicines and tobacco sell the world over. Other of its claims to fame range from D. H. Lawrence to Merry Men, from lace curtains to Trent Bridge cricket and from its castle's great rock to its chemist's glass walls.

Robin Wood lies north-west of the city centre, five minutes' bus ride from the Council House. It is densely built up, though by no means the poorest of the city's artisan quarters. There was a village here as early as the twelfth century. From 1800 onwards the old community and the town of Nottingham seeped up the opposite sides of a separating ridge. The first buildings were terrace houses with attic work-rooms. The houses where the boys and girls of the Enquiry live and one or two little factories tucked alongside them, together with the school (where to-day's youngsters are still being taught) were nearly all put up in a building spate of the 1880's. The streets were named after the local lace masters and textile manufacturers.

The area covered by the Enquiry is a twenty-nine acre block within Robin Wood. It is edged by four traffic-filled roads. Although the fronts of the grander houses (or more accurately the less small ones) are encrusted with fancy brickwork, they are all obviously of the same family. The 900 odd houses are packed so ingeniously into the twenty-nine acres that two people can hardly pass in the entries that divide one set of backs (a shared yard or an eight foot square garden) from those of the parallel street. One of Nottingham's tree-lined boulevards makes a fine flank on the north. Inside the boundary lie twenty-one streets and ten cul-de-sac terraces in which it is estimated that there live 3,700 people of whom 2,149 are adults and 135 are aged fourteen to seventeen. Here therefore, as in other parts of England and

Wales, there is a likelihood that every fifth household will have in it someone of adolescent age. A few small buildings for engineering, printing and woodwork stand cheek by jowl with the houses; but the dominating industrial building is an enormous factory on the opposite side of the western boundary. Robin Wood looks exactly what it is—a late-Victorian working class quarter that has not down-graded itself into tenements, but yet does not display the spit and polish that embellishes a house of one's own. In the words of a local valuer, it is a 'representative area of artisan, two- and three-storied houses, rated at £12–£21 with a rent of 10s. to 12s.; practically none owner-occupied'. While the interviewers did not discover any professional people living actually in the area, only about a fifth of the fathers of the adolescents were unskilled workers. Moreover it is a stable area. Families have often lived here for three generations at least; younger people show little desire to move away when they marry; and so many households have relations living nearby that in Robin Wood private lives are *not* private.

Tightly packed as the houses are, with no bathroom, with their lavatory in the yard, and with a single cold water tap in the scullery, they are not in bad structural condition and only fourteen per cent of Robin Wood residents are applicants for new houses. On the other hand the rooms are extremely cramped and the occupational rate of the neighbourhood is ·62, i.e. four rooms for three people, and five rooms per house. It was found that as many as one in six of the adolescents lived in a household which had eight or more people in it.

Not more than half a dozen of the boys and girls whom the enquirers met lived in the sort of abode where there is no place for anything and nothing ever in it; and there was a corresponding leavening of delightfully spick and span houses. The average Robin Wood home presents a fair face to the world considering the niggardly space, the lack of hot water and the absence of bathrooms. Most front windows show off to-day's brass-and-plaster equivalents of the aspidistra, i.e. dozens of faithful Alsatians, roguish sand-boys and coy cherry-eaters; while a few of the more stylish ones display an aquarium with guppys twitching round their nylon ferns. Well kept or no, there is little space in any of the houses and the living room gets highly congested. The weekly drying and ironing and the daily cooking, the baby, the radio, toddlers, hair washing, homework, pets, toys, visitors, and Dad and Mum have to fit themselves as best they can into a room about twelve feet square. The picture is hackneyed enough, and it is only stressed here because of its obvious bearing on what the adolescent of even a prosperous artisan area is physically able to do inside his home.

Only five streets do not conform to the general pattern. Two of the boundary roads have rather more stylish houses, although these are now mostly shared by several families. Another road is confined to shops of good quality. Off it runs the Tuery, two streets of older houses. They are three-storied terrace houses which still keep the long top floor windows behind which there used to stand the knitter's frame. They also retain their original gardens, the back ones mostly making no pretentions to crops other than mangles, and a dusty hen or two. This and their fence-lessness, reflecting both the physical standards of the Tuery and its unity, make it something of a household word—the sort of place where the kids *would* shove handfuls of earth through your letter box. Some of the streets of bay-windowed houses at the opposite end of the area are regarded as socially superior, but this is probably due to class of tenant and state of repair rather than to the size or the rent of the house. The point to emphasize is that there are steep social gradations within what appears to be so homogeneous a district.

Robin Wood has many small shops inside the area, an 'all sorts' on every corner, a few very second-hand stores, nine off-licenses and an odd bookie or two. These little shops add greatly to the social life and there is not much that the meister and his missus do not know about the local adolescents.

The focal point of the neighbourhood is the intersection of two main roads with traffic lights. This place is known as 'The Cross' and it is the spot to which the boys and girls gravitate at night.

Just off the Cross is a string of public buildings, a church, police station, clinic, library and Grammar School. Within the area is a Primary and Secondary Modern School. In the day-time it is attended by about 380 of the young children of the neighbourhood and about 230 of its older girls, while at night it houses a recreational Evening Institute which teaches chiefly domestic subjects.

A pleasant feature of Robin Wood is its nearness to the Hill, a remnant of Sherwood Forest within three minutes' walk. The Hill is more of a Hampstead Heath than a park. It has attractions for all ages. The new baby and his coach-built pram are taken there for display, toddlers roll in its sandy hollows and seven-year-olds pitch their precarious wigwams on its bosky slopes. Boys on sledges in the winter and on roller-skated boxes at other seasons, hurtle down their Cresta Runs. Maiden ladies exercise their dogs on the Hill, old men smoke their pipes there, and silent huddled couples occupy its benches however dank the night. Religious meetings, cycle races and Goose Fair itself add to the Hill's delights. Thirty-seven of its seventy acres are occupied by football and cricket pitches on hire, by a croquet lawn, bowling and putting greens and by gardeners' sheds. This leaves thirty-three acres of ground that is nominally free and it includes a much-used children's playground. But what with the steepness of part of the land and the inevitable need for re-seeding, any grass site that is large and level enough for a decent if scratch game of football or cricket is rare. A bumpy sand-plus-asphalt portion is the only flat ground that is always available, with the result that the local boys are in constant warfare with the keepers.

Other amenities of Robin Wood include seven solid Victorian pubs. On Friday night, when the week hots up, one of these pubs is the hub of the area. Patrons flow out into the street, kids wriggle up onto the window sills, the piano tinkles, the loudspeaker blares, and the corner fairly hums. Robin Wood also has an unlicensed billiards hall which is open from 10 a.m. to 10 p.m. and is well patronized at its modest charge of fourpence halfpenny the half hour. The major cinema was originally a repertory theatre, and has conserved its robust gilt and mirrors. Just outside the area is another, a typical children and poor mothers' picture palace, with hard and ricketty seats and a serial guaranteed to be of the *Jungle Girl* brand. It has a noisy, enthusiastic audience who wander about and are liable to throw things at each other in a matey way. On Sunday evenings the fourteen and fifteen-year-old boys and girls use it as a kind of club, a spot where they meet crowds of acquaintances and can try their tentative flirtations. Some put off the most tempting alternatives so as not to miss the Palace Sunday show. There are also half-a-dozen cafés of the shake-and-cake brand. Cliques of boys and girls frequent their own particular café and some of the boys always spend the dead hour between Sunday dinner and the five o'clock picture queue in one or other of them.

The children's street life is vigorous. As one child expressed it, 'There's never no time when some isn't not playing in our street'. Certain doorsteps and corners sprout the same set winter and summer, chalking out their hop-scotch and playing an interminable and gambling game of marbles, the profits spent post-haste on ice-lollies. These Robin Wood children play lots of games like 'Tin Can Lurkey' and 'Weak Horse' and 'Slide Box'. Some still bake their own little clay cubes for 'Snobs', just like those excavated on a Roman site on the Fosse, ten miles away. And they can produce rhymes for modern bits of play, like the one for a cigarette packet, 'Willie, Willie Woodbine, Bring me luck, If you don't, I'll tear you up'. Towards the end of October, five or six strongly guarded and handsome guys perched lumpily on corner doorsteps and on the Day itself bonfires blazed in the middle of many of the side streets.

The adult societies range from the strictly local, like the Rose and Crown's Button-Hole Club, to the universal, as represented by the Churches. The Parish Church, which stands just off the Cross, maintains a little Mission Hall, actually inside the Enquiry area. There is another Anglican Church nearby, a Congregational Church at the Cross and in the heart of Robin Wood is a Baptist Church. The latter has no minister and its activities depend largely

PLACE AND PEOPLE   35

on a few hard-working young adults. A community centre just outside the area attracts a few of the parents of the boys and girls; but adults' sports clubs, ex-Servicemen's societies and so on did not crop up much in casual talk. Robin Wood probably resembles most artisan areas in that the majority of its grown-ups belong to no recreational group. Youth organizations are a different matter, though even here it was the interviewer more often than the Robin Wood native who introduced the subject. There is no lack of units, for twelve organizations, specifically for adolescents, meet at least once a week actually within the area; and another two dozen are situated within at most a quarter of an hour's walk. (Appendix II, Table 4.)

The Enquiry only touched the fringe of political societies, but judging from the many notices which appeared during municipal elections, the local Labour Party is an active one. Indeed the Ward's voting figure for the 1950 Municipal election, forty-five per cent, was slightly above the Nottingham average; and in the 1950 Parliamentary election the constituency in which the Ward lies had a voting percentage of eighty-four. It returned a Labour member to Westminster and two Labour and one Liberal representatives to the City Council.

THE BOYS AND THE GIRLS

The above notes have described briefly the districts in which the London and Nottingham boys and girls were living. But people are more important than places, and the following thumbnail sketches of certain of the youngsters (from both villages and towns) may help to introduce their side of the picture. Except that the names are fictitious and that anonymity has demanded certain omissions, the notes stand much as they were written down by the interviewers during the course of the Enquiry.

PAUL (17)

'I had heard from another youngster that this boy's mother was either dead or in a mental hospital, that his elder sister kept house and that he belonged to the Young Communist League. My first visit to him was unfruitful. His sister, a girl of twenty, opened the door and told me Paul was out. She was reluctant to ask me in but finally let me write a note suggesting an appointment to see him later on. When I went again Paul was on the verge of going out and obviously anxious to avoid an interview. His two sisters, the elder about twenty-eight, were sitting at the table which was cluttered with the remains of the evening meal. Paul did eventually sit himself down but the atmosphere was hostile and as he only gave monosyllabic replies I had to talk incessantly to get any conversation going at all. The reason for his suspicions became apparent when he eventually asked "Did you get my name from the Juvenile Court?"

'Gradually I got some information. The father was in hospital with chest trouble and an operation pending. While we were talking a neighbour came in to report on her visit to him. Evidently none of the children were going to see their father that evening. No mention of mother at all. The elder sister kept house as well as holding a job. The second sister had been staying with a relative and had not been back long. It was this girl who had frozen me off on my first visit. She was still wooden and I got the impression that she was very unhappy. The elder one thawed out and became reasonably friendly.

'Paul had been evacuated with the local school. He had been billeted with a woman of sixty who didn't understand children. He was miserable there and had asked for a transfer: but no one bothered to visit him so he just stayed on. He said the local children would not mix with the London ones and that there was a strict dividing line at school and at play. He seemed to be bitter about educational inequalities. He had missed his chance of trying for the scholarship at eleven and I think that this still rankled although he said that a pal of his who had been to a Grammar School had not got a better job than anyone else. Education hadn't done *him* much good, Paul felt.

'Paul is in the building trade, a plasterer. Military service breaks your trade training, he said, and anyhow it contradicted his views as a Communist. He spoke about fighting Malayan Comrades to further American imperialism. The family is R.C. but neither Paul nor the elder girl go to Church. The younger sister said nothing here. When I asked whether his political views clashed with his religion he was emphatic that this was not so. According to him, most youngsters have no fixed views on life. He was very contemptuous of Jack, one of the boys we met who lives in the same buildings. He was equally scornful of Jack's father who had been elected to the Borough Council. He had got in just on his personality, of course. Paul disliked the present M.P. who never came near them during the Election. But he had a high opinion of another and admired the way he stuck to his principles against the Party Whip.

'He does a lot of cycling. Had thought of joining the Y.H.A. but drew back when he found you had to do a job before leaving the hostel in the morning. They should be run properly, he complained, and avoid this sort of thing. Is against gambling—a mug's game. As far as I could make out he divided his time between the Young Communist League and his particular friend, David. He was in the Scouts at one time but gave it up—reason unknown. He took a poor view of the local Mission Clubs, "dirty, gloomy, no discipline". The Community Centre he did approve of, chiefly because it was clean and bright and the company not too rough. Gave no opinion on gangs except that the boys in them are generally too old to be changed, "their minds need reforming". Said membership was largely a family affair—as one boy dropped out another brother took his place. His parting shaft was that he expected this Enquiry would be like other things—nothing would be done as a result of it. He contrasted this with what the Russians did for their young people though he was not in favour of some of the Soviet methods. He even said he might change his mind about Communism; and a friend of his told me later that Paul was less keen than many of the members.

'A difficult shut-in family. Paul himself shied off anything personal. I should imagine he broods a great deal, perhaps on his

Mother. He has probably never known real affection and the right person might do a lot to help him.

'I could not get the schedule filled in.'

JOHN (16)

'A lightly built, pale boy with hair falling into his eyes. Won a place at a Technical School at thirteen. Left at sixteen and is now a carpenter's apprentice on a four year agreement. Attended Day Release Classes at a College of Further Education. Has been in the job for nearly five months. Likes it and aspires to be a carpenter in a big firm.

'We met John at his home. He made no objections to the questions put to him, though his replies were somewhat difficult to catch because of a broken voice and a stout accent. He had earned some money from a paper round while he was still at school, had never belonged to a juvenile organization nor a Sunday School, but was now a member of a Pigeon Club. Had begun to keep pigeons when he was twelve. He and his mate, a seventeen-year-old boy, were the Club's youngest members. He said that they were always discussing the birds. Two of his pigeons had won prizes at recent shows and another had taken third place against two hundred bird competitors in a Doncaster race. He produced the prize cards.

'We saw his twenty birds in their open air shed at the bottom of the garden, handsome creatures which had cost £2 to £5 apiece. Some he had reared himself. We also inspected their travelling basket, acquired second-hand. His mother told us that he had lost five birds in flights, including one which had just managed to reach the garden hedge and had then collapsed. It had been shot. The whole pigeon outfit was extremely well cared for and was obviously an absorbing and expensive interest.

'John's other hobbies were autocycling and pigs. He had bought himself a £27 machine and was rearing the pigs to raise the cash to repay what he had borrowed for the cycle. In the evenings he either rode off on this, with his mate, or wandered around with a gang of buddies, all aged under seventeen. He went to the pictures occasionally but only when he knew the film was worth seeing. On one evening in the week he reckoned to stay in looking at T.V. and reading up his pigeons. He generally went to bed between ten and eleven o'clock and was out of the house in the morning by a quarter past seven.

'Finally we inspected the three pigs which John greeted in a familiar way though he confided that his father helped to look after them as he himself was pressed for time. The pigs, some rabbits and a ferret concluded his livestock.'

EILEEN (17)

'I was unable to get asked in and had to sit on the house steps to fill in the schedule. Eileen seemed to think the Enquiry a great waste of her time and her one thought was to speed it up. She comes in from work, gets smartened up and goes out, apparently to hang around the streets though I could not be sure if she was telling me the truth. I should not think there is much comfort in her home from what she says.

'When she left school a friend told Eileen about a possible job at the former's firm. Eileen went off after it by herself and took it as she wanted to work where there was someone whom she knew. I suspect she has changed jobs more times than she admitted. She said her present work was all right but that she would leave if something better turned up. According to her there are no decent clubs in the area and when I asked her about a neighbouring district she laughed and said she never went there; but again I felt she was answering with her tongue in her cheek. Dislikes coloured people, and would hate them to touch her. Never thinks about religion, has too much else to do. Believes there is a God but the subject doesn't enter her mind unless she is frightened. Leisure to her means spending money, and work earning it.'

BILL (15)

'A square-set forthright, apple-cheeked individual. Has an extraordinarily harsh voice, toned down by a genial grin. Sports a canary-yellow polo sweater and looks like an immature edition of what he will probably become, a competent Mine Host. A masterful boy who already likes to rule the roost at his home which is comfortable and relatively empty as it has only two children, Bill and his nine-year-old sister.

'Had an excellent junior school record ("an 'A' boy, smart, a fighter, a worker") and was top of the form for three years at his secondary modern school. A reader, too, and at fourteen kept his own record book. He classed *Elizabeth and Philip* as "fair", *Association Football for Boys* as "very good", and *Black Beauty* as "excellent". Has some dramatic talent and was a convincing pirate in the school play. His ruling passion was, and is, football. He plays for the school and attends every home match of the city team. He watches these from the children's pen to which he is entitled as a member of the Supporters' Club. Takes sandwiches and his sister.

'Football is not his only interest as is shown by his replies to the schedule on how he had spent his spare time in the seven preceding days.

' "Yesterday I went to the pictures with my friend Bill Hardy—a gangster film—very good. The day before I listened to the wireless and played a cricket game called Howzat. The day before I cycled to a village just outside D. with my friend Charles. The day before I went to the Speedway track with my next door neighbour who has a car. The day before I finished some homework for school, did some odd jobs, washed the pots and cleaned my bike. On Saturday I finished my delivery job in the morning, then watched a good cricket match. On Sunday I went on my bike with a man friend from across the road, looked the town over, had some lunch and got back at 4.30 p.m. after a forty mile run." '

PHYLLIS (15)

'A counter hand. Parents dead. Lives with her grandfather and grandmother. A younger brother and sister are in orphanages and another sister lives with friends. My impression was that Phyllis was not very happy. Her grandparents would like her to stay at home in the evenings but home has not much attraction. They are out of sympathy with a young girl, she resents their authority and pines for younger people. She would like to live on her own, she said, in a flat with nice furniture. I should imagine that the line she takes as an adult will depend on what acquaintances she makes within the next year or two. Has never belonged to any clubs.'

JUNE (17)

'Sweet seventeen at its least hackneyed. Pretty frocks, a piquant face, warm-hearted, spontaneous. Is willing to shoulder responsibility too. Thinks a great deal of a club she happened upon two years ago when, as she alleges, she was a shy blushful girl who stayed at home and did not think about anything much except other girls, sweets and knitting. The club loosened her tongue and opened new worlds to her—the theatre, concerts, youth hostels, badminton, and above all new and exciting friends.

'Is warmly attached to her mother who delights in the girl's many outside activities, vets them on occasion, but leaves her much freedom.'

SIDNEY (17)

'Sidney's mother is a kindly person not unduly swamped by her nine children, of whom Sidney is the fifth. She always had time to help with the Enquiry, was sympathetic towards her boys' interest in sport and encouraged them to belong to youth groups. Sidney was a steady member of one organization or another from the time he was five. Was in St. John's Sunday School Cubs and Scouts until he was fourteen. Then he went to a Boys' Brigade, then to a boys' Club, then to a Free Church Youth Club, and now, at seventeen, he has joined a more go-ahead Church Club. None of this membership has overlapped and he seems to have changed from one to another society for sensible reasons. In two cases the organization disbanded and in a third the group was definitely below his own standards. He never seems to have been in one of the usual tight cliques of boys. Possibly he makes friends easily but at a not very deep level and prefers the casual friendships of an organization to those of a smaller circle. All his societies except one have been connected with a Church. He was one of the few youngsters who volunteered that they were interested in religion. At the moment he is going through a typical questioning stage.

'All the boys of his family are sportsmen, as he is himself. Plays cricket and football seriously and if he were earning more it would go on a new football and football boots. If he had the time he would see more 1st Division matches and go to the swimming baths oftener.

'He is an engineering apprentice and enjoys the job but makes what sound like valid criticisms on his charge-hand. Two days in the week he works a twelve-hour shift and is very fatigued after it.

'A steady, reliable, open boy, much attached to his home and to the neighbourhood.'

GLADYS (15)

'In a fairly high grade at school. Has had three jobs since leaving. Is now with a shoe manufacturer "putting silver paper on cardboard".

'Our interview was carried out on the doorstep with various members of the family and neighbours listening in. Mother slovenly looking. Younger children untidily dressed. Gladys's own clothes were grubby and she had nicotined fingers (she came to the door smoking). But she is an attractive girl with natural curls and pretty colouring. The house, a shared one, was as dilapidated looking as its occupants. The girls sleep together of course.

'Gladys seems to live her own life without much parental control. Would like to have more money for the clothes which she so patently does not know how to look after. Had thought of going to evening classes for dressmaking but gave up the idea. No special boy friend she said, although she likes to go out with boys. Does not know what she and her friend Jessica will do in the winter evenings but expects that they will still go out for walks "just the same". Reckons to go to the pictures two or three times a week and always roller skates on Saturday night. As a school girl used to be very keen on swimming, but never swims now. Gladys was conversant with youth organizations as she had been a Guide when she was about twelve and later had belonged to a club, just for a month or two. She found it dull, and left. Might try a club again if one started up near her home, especially if there was dancing at it.'

TED (17) AND SAMMY (15)

'These brothers, one a shop assistant and the other, by his own account, a "cinema poster-writer", shared one passion—birds. Anything connected with woods, fields, and ponds delighted them. A family taste apparently, for Ted inherited a Victorian tome on natural history from his grandfather. Their father, too, from the time the boys were tiny, used to take them off to the country on Sundays on his motor bike. But they have always lived in a large town.

'They began to concentrate on birds when Ted was fifteen. Sammy even left the Scouts about this time, much as he enjoyed their camping. But knots and so on were dull stuff compared with the new hobby. He dropped out of a boxing club that he quite enjoyed for the same reason. "We couldn't afford to waste time from the birds, we had so much to do." They even went to the extraordinary length, for most of the youngsters, of *buying* books—7s. 6d. affairs like Seaton Thompson's *British Birds' Eggs*—and indeed began to write their own, of which the following is an extract: "Sunday 14th May, 1950. We set off about 8.30 a.m. for D. We had been off the bus about one hour when we found the semi-domed nest of the chiff-chaff. The nest contained four eggs. Strangely enough it was over 200 yards from the nearest water. Later we came across a yellow bunting's nest with young. After hearing the laughing cry of the green woodpecker we decided to go into the woods and try and locate its nest. To our surprise we found a nuthatch's nest in an old nesting box, the eggs laid on the almost bare box. On the outside of the wood we found a partridge guarding her clutch. Feeling a bit tired I sat down to rest. A bird flew from almost underneath me and parting the grass I found a tree pipit's nest with two eggs. Later on in the afternoon we found a robin's nest in a tin. This contained two eggs and a young cuckoo. Making our way to the bus stop we found a barn owl up a tree. We decided to have a closer look, and so Sam climbed up. The bird did not stir until Sam could almost touch it, then fluttered to the ground. I picked up the bird, saw that it had one eye missing, and was weak with hunger. We took it home to give to the P.D.S.A."

'Later on, the two boys, together with a third, became madly keen on week-end cycling expeditions to the country, with equipment that consisted of a tent, a frying pan and quantities of tins. Their mother was apprehensive, but they survived. Finally Ted joined the Y.H.A. and within the first six months had sampled six hostels. Sammy started to breed cage birds and began to dream of owning a pet shop.'

FRANCES (16)

'Has had four jobs and is now a chocolate packer. Says her family all marry early. Her brother was eighteen when he got married and her sister was not quite twenty. All her friends have ambition to marry before long, Frances says, and a lot of girls she used to go with married when they were about eighteen.

'I saw her Dad, a cheerful chap in the forties. Looked like a builder's labourer but hadn't done anything about his own house which was paintless outside and, from the little I saw, a hugger-mugger place within. I did not meet her mother. Her father said he had no influence over Frances. The latter did not seem to have much personality and I doubt if any youth organizations could compete successfully with her home.'

ESMÉ (15)

A well set-up, trimly dressed young woman, who looks more like a girl in work than at school. Her home is super-tidy, and

Esmé the only child. Father a mechanic. Mother works part-time and Esmé hopes to get into the offices of the latter's firm. Has been at a Grammar School since she was eleven and is now in the commercial form. This means that she has no homework (and incidently has had no physical training or games for the last twelve months). Is longing for the day when she can leave. This was the attitude she took when she was first interviewed and she held to it later. There is no lesson that she really enjoys. She has never identified herself with the school's social life. Neither of her two friends is a grammar school girl.

'Has been in a Church set for years. Belonged to its Guides and Sunday School and became a class teacher at fourteen. Now, at fifteen and a half, she has suddenly dropped out of Guides, has finished with Sunday School and has sprung a passion for dancing. She goes with a much older girl every Friday and sometimes, rather guiltily, on a Sunday. Seems to have felt that the Church activities were children's affairs which she was obliged to shake off if she was ever to grow up. Dancing of course is definitely an adult activity. Very boy-conscious.'

BERT RICHARDSON (16)

'Everyone in Daltons Buildings knows the Richardsons, there is such a packet of them. The night the Census was taken there were eleven sleeping at home, one son with his wife and child was living across the road, a similar trio were a few streets away and the others were who knows where? Mr. Richardson is a brawny man, a labourer and ex-sailor, rough but amicable. He follows sport and is intensely proud of various of his sons' sporting successes. The boys' cups, plaques and prize cards pretty well furnish the front room mixed up with a sofa full of loaves, the day's bread intake. Mr. Richardson knows a good deal about the local youth organizations and thinks highly of the leader of a club that his boys have belonged to.

'His wife is gaunt, grey, lined and laconic. She must be extraordinarily strong for, with the sixteen children she has reared and the eleven to keep house for, she is now, at fifty-five, starting to go out to work part-time. And her house is ship-shape too, in a rough-and-ready fashion.

'Bert comes about the middle of the family and is an uncouth, unvocal chap but no dunderhead. The interviewer put him on the defensive at once as he suspected he was trying to get him back into a club he had lately abandoned. Almost the only sliver of information about his leisure that a series of interviewers ever extracted from Bert himself was that of course he went to the pictures, who didn't?

'School had rated Bert as no scholar and only gave him a "C" for health or appearance. But he soared to the "A's" for behaviour, "a likeable lad and a splendid worker, honest and trustworthy".

'The Richardson boys ganged up with two other big families in their buildings. At various ages their gangs had tried out most of the local youth organizations. Bert, with a suitable set of brothers and mates was in the Scouts at one time but they got ejected. Later, at thirteen, he joined a boys' club for its boxing and football. He never attended regularly and was always behindhand with his subs, but he belonged on and off until he was about sixteen. Then he suddenly gave up boxing (his family didn't know the reason) and dropped out of the club. The leader hit the nail on the head when he said of Bert that while he was never the correct member he probably got a lot out of the Club.'

ELSIE (17)

'An only child who always manages to look like the heroine of the serial in this week's *Woman*.

'She went from a Secondary Modern School into clerical work and stayed there for two years, i.e. from fourteen to sixteen. She did not get on with those in authority and was moved to several departments to see if she would fit in better. Finally she was dismissed for a defiant attitude. She moved to another firm where she did the same kind of work and this time got on excellently. Nothing accounted for the change except that the final rumpus with the first firm occurred soon after she had made a boy-friend.

'Elsie was never one for social contacts though she was in a Sunday School up to the time she met her boy friend and she had been a Brownie as a small child. But she refused to go up into the Guides because she had loved the Brownies so dearly. This was typical of her liking for few but very close attachments. The only girl friend she ever acquired got engaged on her sixteenth birthday and was married at seventeen. Elsie herself started courting when she was fifteen and a half, from which time she centred her energies on her boy and on getting married. This she did when she was just eighteen. Her leisure-time, recorded for two separate weeks, the first five months before she married and the second nine months later, gives some indication of how her life was oriented.

	Week 1.	*Week 2.*
Mon.	Went to sea-side (on my boy's motor-bike)	Knitting and write to my husband
Tues.	Can't remember	Embroidery ,, ,,
Wed.	Trip to F. (with my boy)	Ironing ,, ,,
Thurs.	Out on motor-bike (with my boy)	Mother's ,, ,,
Fri.	Dancing (with my boy)	
Sat.	Shopping in afternoon. To friend's relations in the evening	*Morn.* Washing *Aft.* At my mother's *Eve.* At home again. Write to my husband
Sun.	Cooking in the morning. Walk in the evening (with my boy)	*Morn.* Mend stockings *Eve.* Sister-in-law's and write to my husband

RAYMOND (17)

'Raymond is a much more able boy than most I met. He is a glib quick talker who would rather act than think. He is much attracted to men of action and I suspect would be easily influenced by any forceful character, bad or good. He said himself that if he could get the right girl it would be a good thing for him. I did not much like his attitude to his parents. He was patronizing and I should think they have never had much control over the boy. They seem in easy circumstances and their flat is comfortable.

'None of the family go to Church nor has Ray any feelings about religion. He has no colour prejudice and knows and likes a number of the foreigners of the neighbourhood. Lots of the local mixed marriages are happy, he says, and if he saw a coloured girl he fancied he would certainly go out with her.

'He was in the Scouts from eleven to thirteen, left them to join the Army Cadets but dropped out after three months because it was boring and because he did not get the chance to go to camp. He joined a Recreational Institute too, but he gave it up after a fight with some boys who were cocky to him. He knew quite a lot about youth organizations and I asked for his comments. He had one major criticism, that it was always the grown-ups and never the boys who really ran the show. He then expatiated on a private club that some of the boys in his street had founded. His mother let them use the front room (it wasn't furnished) and they could box there and play indoor games. The leader had obviously been Raymond. It was just the sort of situation that he would enjoy. His neighbourhood abounds in boys who revel in this sort of position so long as it involves them in no responsibility.

'When he was younger he was interested in camping, P.T., boxing and carpentry. Now that he is seventeen he has two main leisure-time occupations. He tries to raise money by any side line he can invent and he looks over the girls.'

ROSIE (16)

'A pretty, gentle, pink-and-white creature. Should have been a shepherdess but to-day minds her machines. Has three elder and five younger brothers and sisters. Their little home was always packed but it invariably had a welcome and practical help for the outsider. The household seemed on remarkably good terms with each other. Teachers recalled that all the children of this family were sensible, solid and well-mannered and that Rosie, a plodder in the practical class, was nevertheless a mother to the little ones.

'She was sent off to Sunday School as a little girl, as a matter of course, and she was a Guide from the time she was eleven until she was fourteen. But even as a school girl she didn't link up with any set, she just kept to one friend at a time. In the same way, her adolescent friendships concentrated on just one person, a girl who lived nearby. The two worked together and spent most of the time they were not busy with chores at home in making contact with the local boys. They made use of the pictures, of dances and of 'up the street' for this purpose—all in a discreet but diligent way. They had no false shame about it and planned to marry at nineteen or twenty. Her family background suggested that Rosie would probably be an active member of some youth organization, since both her father and mother were stalwarts of a local political party and of various social and sports clubs. In actual fact, Rosie had no use for youth organizations at all. She regarded them as somewhat alien societies, composed of girls with whom she had no particular wish to associate. The organizations made no appeal to her good nature as they did not directly ask her to do something for somebody else, the sort of call to which she would probably have responded. So, as she was genuinely shy, she concentrated on her single friendship. In any case she saw this as a suitable medium for promoting her main interest, the acquisition of a serious boy friend.' (Interviewers' note, a year later, 'Is now engaged'.)

HARRY (17)

'A boy with a constant and absorbing passion—cycle racing. Harry's father had been in the Cyclists' Touring Club as a young fellow and had introduced Harry's mother, then a girl of eighteen, to cycling. After they were married they used to take the babies with them on their cycling expeditions. They gave Harry his first bike when he was fourteen. He joined a cycling club at fifteen and the same year entered for his first race. At the time of the Enquiry he was racing regularly, riding with a flock of cyclists most Sundays, and by himself or with a mate nearly every week night. He was training hard, winning a gratifying number of events and spending most of his free time and money on the one hobby. His diary reads like this:

Sunday (*April* 1950). Club run 9 a.m. Lovely morning for a ride. Had dinner at E. After dinner we made our way slowly to the tea place at C. We arrived there early so we had a good game of football. The Club left the tea place at 6.30 p.m. and arrived home at 9 p.m. Total mileage, about 89 miles.

Monday. Training with a few club mates. Went to the Blue Bell Café. I spent 1s. there. Arrived home 9.15 p.m.

Tuesday. Clubroom 8 p.m. Had a good game of table-tennis. Spent 9d. in the canteen. Entered the Club 50-mile Time Trial for next Sunday. Entrance fee 2s. 6d. Got home at 9.45 p.m.

Wednesday. Went training with a few clubmates. Mileage 39 miles.

Thursday. Went training on my own tonight. One of my clubmates has had the 'flu' so he can't come.

Saturday. Asked my clubmate to bring me a new sou'wester as I'd bought a cape the week before. It cost me 4s 6d.

Sunday. Went racing with the Club. Fifty-mile Time Trial. Entrance fee 2s. 6d. I finished about 12th. My time was 2 hours, 29 minutes, 13 seconds. I came home for dinner then went out with the Club for tea. Tea cost 2s. 3d. We had poached egg on toast, cakes and tea. We arrived home at 9.30 p.m. 98 miles.

Harry's job, a routine factory one where he was earning about 52s. a week at sixteen, seldom came into his conversation though his foreman spoke quite well of him. He was a Scout from twelve to fourteen. According to the Troop, he left because of some row with the band-master; by his own account because it was all talk and no do. He and his pals had wanted to play at things they made up for themselves and not all to do the same things at the same time. He pointed out that in the cycling club you were not over-controlled. People of all ages and both sexes belonged which made the company more interesting than one of boys only. Harry was on good terms with his parents and with his two younger brothers. He had plenty of interests, quite an ear for classical music and was even a reader in a small way. He rather liked girls but a serious one would have diverted cash and time from the bike, so he had decided to keep heart-free.'

HAROLD (17)

'Mother in hospital for the last year with nervous trouble. No information about father. Boy a G.P.O. telephone engineer much above the average in intelligence and tastes. Not a prig, just serious-minded.

'Filled up the schedule himself with precise answers. Reads anything, Jules Verne, Shaw, Wells, Flaubert, and enjoys talking about books. Keen on music. Stays in on Monday nights for radio plays and would like to go to the theatre but cannot find anyone else who wants to go. Enjoys the cinema but seldom finds enough time for it.'

SALLY (17)

'Sally comes from a family that has had to reverse itself as far as earning a living goes. Her father has worked in various jobs, in glass and lace factories, and as a builder. Then he went into the Army. He contracted T.B. and has been in bed for the last sixteen months. His wife, therefore, has to work and goes off each day at four o'clock. Sally herself gets in from work at a quarter past six, gets a meal for her father and small brother, puts the latter to bed, and generally sees after the home. She has to do a good deal of housework at the week-end. In addition to this, to eke out her pocket money, she helps her father with any small packaging work that he is able to do at home.

'She is a pleasant, homely sort of girl, wears no make-up and looks younger than her age. As a small child she had not very much confidence in herself and was in the practical class at school. She returned the school's opinion of her abilities by saying that her last year there, from fourteen to fifteen, was a waste of time. Once she started work however, as a machinist in a tailoring firm, she got on well. She is called an apprentice and is prepared, with some pressure from her father, to stick at this job although she gets relatively low wages. She wants a trade behind her for later on. It means that she only gets seven shillings a week pocket money.

'She is not much of a mixer. As a school child she used to play with some other little girls, but she sees nothing of them now although they still live in neighbouring streets. Her companion is a boy three years younger than herself whom she started to befriend when he lost his father a year ago. It is a real children's friendship. Sometimes they go to the pictures together, but their main activity is cycling. Exploring new places on her bike is Sally's main interest.

'Her father and mother have taken a lot of care with Sally and are a little worried that she does not make friends of her own age. Her mother was in the Guides as a girl and thinks that a youth organization would give Sally a little more self confidence. She is not really a recluse but as yet she lacks the courage to take the plunge of facing a new group. She is such a likeable, good-hearted girl that some society really ought to have the benefit of her company.'

ARTHUR (16)

'A slightly built, sharp-featured boy with bright brown eyes and a shy manner. Like a squirrel. Looks nearer fourteen than almost seventeen. Artistic. In a factory job. Is the second of seven children whose ages range from four to twenty-three. Six live at home. Arthur's activities centre round a street group of seven boys aged thirteen to sixteen. Within this set he has one particular friend whom he has known since they were five and who, although he now lives two miles away, comes up to the street three or four time a week. All the set have bikes. They go off to the woods for the day on Saturdays and Sundays, or go fishing in twos and threes. They play a lot of scratch football and finish up perhaps three times a week at the pictures. If one is hard up the others raise his ticket money.

'Arthur seems to have done no more than cast an eye at the local youth organizations and doesn't much like talking about them. He did go for a few weeks to a Scout troop just across the road, and also to a boys' club. So far as one can guess from what he did and did not say, both these organizations were overcontrolled for the taste of a shy and rather sensitive boy. He made one point, that he liked young fellows as leaders better than a middle-aged man.'

MARIA (18)

'Parents both Italian. Father dead. Mother speaks only broken English. House very poor and ill-kept but Maria has been to a convent boarding school and has acquired cultural interests. Has hardly any friends in the district as most of her childhood was spent at the convent. Those she has are all older and were met through her job as a telephonist. Would be interested to join either a dramatic or a sports club if there was a suitable one in the district but she feels she cannot make her friends locally. Since no one at work shares her high falutin' interests she does not pursue them. An intelligent, self-possessed girl trying hard to better herself.'

TED

'Ted is an electrician's mate. He is one of the boys of good intelligence who does not now belong to any organization although he was in the Scouts for a year when he was eleven, and later on, for a short period, in two clubs. He lives alone with his mother in the top two rooms of a tenement house which is in very bad condition. The back room was previously Ted's room but it is now so damp and insanitary that he and his mother have to sleep in the sitting room. They have a small gas cooker on the landing and a sink on the landing below. Ted's father died when he was three and he has been brought up by his mother. She works as a cleaner. She is in very poor health, and has something wrong with her heart as well as chronic bronchitis. They obviously have a struggle to make ends meet. Ted's supper, the night I was there, was a couple of thick slices of bread with a few fried onions on it. This background has, I think, moulded Ted's character and attitude to life. He is a quiet boy and was suspicious to begin with; but became friendly when he realized that I wanted his help and was not working against his interests in any way.

'Ted doesn't appear to do much thinking for himself. He likes being in a group and doing things with them. He left various youth clubs because his pals did. Apart from the cinema and reading twopenny bloods, his main interest is football, which I believe he plays well. He is keen on other sports but to a lesser degree. He criticized youth clubs for their amateurish approach to sport, and their low standard of achievement. He said that he would like to belong to a club that concentrated on sport, and whose standard of play was high. He and his pals didn't like being bossed around. He thought that clubs didn't *do* enough, or rather make it possible for the boys to *do* enough things. He went camping once with the Scouts. The boys weren't permitted outside the field except with the leader or for some special activity as a Troop, whereas Ted would have liked to explore the countryside by himself. He said he wished he could get into the country now sometimes but he couldn't afford a bike or the high fares.

'He has no special liking for working near home and one of the attractions of his present job is the fact that he travels around. Neither he nor his mother go to Church and he had no feeling about religion; he is just not interested. A number of coloured families live nearby and he said all the boys of the street play quite happily together. Both he and his mother liked the coloured people they knew.

'He didn't strike me as being particularly happy. I think in a negative kind of way he felt that his life wasn't very purposeful. He hadn't bothered to find out the conditions of work in his present employment and didn't know whether or not he got any annual holiday. I think his bad living conditions and the feeling of responsibility for his sick mother weighed him down and depressed him. Whenever his mother started talking about her troubles he closed up and it was difficult to start him talking again.'

• • •

PASSING THE TIME

In trying to discover why the boys and girls did or did not join a youth group, the enquirers amassed a jumble of facts on how these particular representatives of the generation that was born just before the War elected to use their leisure. The facts were not too difficult to get at but it was extraordinarily hard to assess the actual quality of the youngsters' activities. To proclaim against the more obvious faults was easy; but it was a different matter to say what really would have been a sound leisure for those of so different an age, upbringing and occupation from that of their assessors. The latter only ventured on an appraisement in the belief that, since their observation was at heart friendly, this might ward off too many false judgments.

The Nottingham interviewers, from their first superficial contacts with the boys and girls, noticed a marked variety in the way they elected to pass their non-working hours. Two boys of much the same age, social level and school class would spend their free time in entirely different ways. The tastes of one boy had obviously matured, while the other was content to go on doing at seventeen just about what he had done when he was fifteen. Some were self-sufficient, and could enjoy themselves by themselves, on occasion. Others panicked at the idea of having to undertake anything alone. Some led a gregarious life, while certain ones had hardly any friends among their contemporaries, none at all of the opposite sex, and even shied off older people for anything more than the essential contacts. Certain of the youngsters led a strangely self-centred existence, while others, though most of them met their home obligations manfully, were apparently never asked to lift a finger for anyone outside the family circle.

Circumstances, of course, as well as personality, determined their leisure-time occupations. Health was one of the obvious conditioners. Indifferent health, particularly in the 'poor' home, often tied the adolescent boy or girl to one or other parent. Those whose leisure was noticeably stereotyped tended to look below par physically. Certain of the less robust and mentally slow girls seemed to use up most of their powers in coping with the daily round. Any extra energy they possessed probably went in prospecting around, in a mild way, for a husband.

Parental rulings were still surprisingly strict in many homes, especially as to the hour a daughter had to be in the house at night. Domestic obligations were frequent. 'Always the ironing on Tuesdays' or 'helping my father at night with the accounts' were typical jobs. The tools a youngster could lay hands on and, perhaps more important, the amount of free space in his home and yard, directly affected what he did with his after-work hours. Lack of elbow room had been an obstacle to creative leisure for most of these youngsters all their lives. They had never had guaranteed privacy, nor sustained quiet, nor space for using tools, nor safe storage for their wet, fragile and sticky-odoriferous creations and collections. Except for the rare home which definitely encouraged indoor play, their hobbies had been constantly under comment from someone's hand or tongue. In the tidy Nottingham home tradition, too, was a handicap, for the front room was kept sacred even in summer, and in winter any bad weather that brought the kids in early from the street meant that the living room became even more congested than usual.

Hobbies do not develop in a vacuum; and grown-ups often influenced the pursuits of the rising generation. Moreover, when a youngster's uncle or sister-in-law did take an interest, they probably reinforced this with tools—a fishing rod perhaps, or a solid £5 towards the B.S.A. motor-bike. Nor was it just a case of contiguous generations. The hobby might rove back to a great-grandparent; and those which were traditional in the family commanded respect and held their own sturdily against the somewhat fleeting activities of many of the youth organizations.

Money is alleged to affect directly the way in which adolescents spend their time. In Nottingham the boys did not appear to handle more pocket money than the girls; and the sexes seemed to live at much the same economic level. The Grammar School pupils, on the other hand, were noticeably hard-up compared to their more affluent age-mates at work. Despite this their leisure-time occupations showed more variety. The really significant point about the spending power of those at work was that it was always rising (Appendix II, Table 5c). The minute calculations of cost of

PLACE AND PEOPLE 57

their early days no longer hindered them from gratifying their tastes; as soon as they started to earn they were for ever being enabled to buy more satisfactions, and dearer ones. Most of them did this, of course. But relatively few bought new *kinds* of experience as they grew older; and this was more often due to lack of a ruling passion than to shortage of cash.

Fairly detailed information was collected in all the areas as to how specific boys and girls spent their leisure. In London about 165 of the Northbury adolescents provided a record of how they had spent the evenings of the seven preceding days. Their answers were arbitrarily classified into 'desultory' (64), 'home-centred' (31), 'organized' (50), 'evening classes' (11), 'individual purposes' (9). The 'desultory' meant walking around, playing on bombed sites, cycling, and two or three visits to the cinema. 'Home centred' included housework, reading and the wireless. 'Organized' and 'evening classes' meant that several evenings a week had been spent at some formal group. Any evening occupied with what sounded like a genuine hobby was listed under 'individual purposes'. The boys were keen on football, swimming, cricket, and table-tennis in roughly that order. Several unofficial football teams which they played in were mentioned. One, to the concern of some parents, met in a pub. These informal teams were almost always handicapped by lack of local pitches and by the players' reluctance to travel beyond a very short distance for mere scratch games. Any level ground, a yard, a side street, or a bombed site, was made use of.

In Camdington, likewise, sport was the boys' major interest, especially football. Here again they were limited by lack of grounds and by their own prejudice against mobility, though in Camdington the boys were sometimes able to get pitches in the local parks and official open spaces. Fishing was surprisingly popular, perhaps because of the proximity of a canal and ponds. A few complete anglers went even further afield. The girls, on the other hand, had hardly any facilities for their type of games. Apart from swimming baths they were much less well catered for than the boys. Nor, of course, did they get the dinner hour exercise, such as kicking a ball about the factory yard, that so many of the boys enjoyed. The younger girls made many requests for more opportunities for outdoor games and for such a facility as a gymnasium. There was also some demand for inexpensive classes in ballroom dancing. One of the more popular ways of spending an evening was to go dancing, but in general the girls did not reckon to dance more than once or twice a week. A cycling craze was on at the time of the Enquiry; and a large proportion of both boys and girls had the use of a bicycle. Indeed, a cycle was regarded as essential for making street encounters, since it is quite in order to pick up boys if one is on a bike—an altogether different matter from going after them on foot. Energetic cycling was almost unknown; what so many of them mentioned was a strictly local activity. Lastly there were the indoor pastimes; but it was summer when the Enquiry took place and they were not much in evidence. Only a small number of the boys had any such definite hobby as model aeroplanes, stamps, pigeons, tropical fish and so on. The difficulties of pet keeping (with all the Council regulations to conform to) were stressed on several occasions. Music was the one art which just a few did pursue. Several were having piano lessons and one or two possessed a gramophone. On the few evenings when the youngsters were in the house the wireless got half an ear, but no one stayed in to listen to a particular programme. Hardly any of the London homes had as yet got a television set.

In Nottingham 55 boys and 62 girls gave an account of how they spent the evenings of the seven days preceding that on which they were interviewed. The details are given in Appendix II, Table 5a.

Courting and going to the pictures were two ways of spending time that recurred constantly in the records from town and country alike. Another way of occupying leisure, book reading, drew attention to itself only by its absence. The bald question 'What do you read?' is so liable to misinterpretation that it was not included in the schedule. But incidental information picked up here and there in Central London and in Nottingham suggested

that relatively few of the youngsters ever read a book as such.*
Only 24 of 159 Northbury boys and girls held a ticket at a Public
Library, while in Robin Wood, where there was a very attractive
library within five minutes' walk, only 38 out of 129 youngsters
were ticket holders in 1950, and this had dropped to 25 in the
following year. Most of the Robin Robin Wood boys and girls
did read a local evening paper however, and a smaller number
sampled some national paper such as the *Daily Mirror*. They also
read the more lurid Sunday Press; and any home which took
several Sunday papers regarded this as a matter for pride. Their
next bulk of reading was magazines—sporting, film, feminine
and science-fiction—followed by a legion of paper-backed *Crime-
Detectives*. These magazines were not necessarily ephemeral reading, since some of them, as e.g. *Illustrated*, included easy-to-read
technical material. But many of the magazines they read, and
especially their comics, could not claim to be anything but time-
killers for those as old as sixteen and seventeen. Comics indeed
formed almost the sole reading of certain of the adolescents. They

* READING
NOTTINGHAM—Robin Wood

	Reading for previous night	Reading in general
Boy 17	Nothing	Nothing
Girl 16	*Nottingham Eve. Post*	Evening Paper
Girl 16	*Nottingham Eve. Post & Nottingham Eve. News*	Evening Papers
Girl 15	Nothing	Magazines (*Woman's Own, Red Star*)
Boy 15	*Nottingham Eve. Post*	Evening Paper
Girl 16	Nothing	Books for school work; not much general reading
Girl 17	Nothing	Magazines (*Red Letter, Woman's Own,*
Girl 17	Nothing	Comics (*Dandy, Beano, Superman*), *Graphic, Reveille, Evening News,* 5 Sunday Papers, *True Stories*
Boy 15	Nothing	*Nottingham Eve. Post, Daily Mirror, Despatch, Pictorial, Football Post*
Boy 16	*Black Death* (Book)	*Nottingham Eve. Post, News of the World, Sunday Express, People, Empire*

still bothered to read regularly the *Dandys* and *Radio Fun* that they had been buying and swopping over since they were old enough to interpret the drawings, and added to them the newer 6*d*. and 1*s*. American publications (or British editions of American ones) aimed at the reader who is adult in years. Sufficient calumny has been piled onto the comics to deter this Report from adding its straw, except to point out that many of their particular devotees were strapping young men and women who had *not* outgrown their *Spymasters* and *Dixie Dungans* as children are alleged to do.

Why were so few of these adolescents able to get any pleasure from books? In the first place, if they had been book readers they would have been pioneers since the adults of their world on the whole did not read books. This was self-evident from the absence of books and book-shelves in the boys' and girls' homes, and from the character of the literature on sale locally. Seven of the hundred or so shops in the immediate vicinity of Robin Wood, with its two thousand adults, sold reading matter. But, by one morning's search, their total stock of books (apart from children's) was three *Penguins*, a dictionary, a *Mrs. Dale's Diary* and about ten Whodunits.

It was obvious that the boys and girls seldom heard books talked about, they did not read the kind of newspapers that refer to books, they hardly ever went into a genuine bookshop, and they were obviously at sea as to *what* was suitable when, as happened occasionally, they rather fancied a 'thick' book. Moreover, while pen and ink are necessary for the important business of letter writing and still retain some mystique, many of these youngsters' homes obviously regarded a mere reader as a time-waster, especially if a feminine one. Add to this the physical hindrances, the distraction of the wireless as well as the interruptions that are inevitable in a living room which is used by the whole household. Add, too, that few of the youngsters had a haven in the shape of a bedroom of their own. The very mechanics of reading still bothered some, though in Robin Wood only one adolescent, a boy of sixteen, was too illiterate even to make out page one of *Benjamin Bunny*. But there were a good many others who jibbed at the long, long page of solid print which a book normally presupposes. Perhaps the real trouble went deeper. In the first place books smacked of school. They were childish, old fashioned stuff that was below the adolescent's new status as a wage earner. And if these youngsters were determined about anything it was that their pleasures should be modern. Moreover solid reading is a solitary business, and most of the boys and girls could not face being alone, or rather did not conceive that it was possible to enjoy oneself alone.

It may be that the new media of hearing and seeing in wireless and television, rather than the old one of reading, will make the educated man of the future. Possibly the generation of near-adults whom the interviewers met was reflecting the change-over, though television had not yet reached a large enough number of homes to justify comment. The ubiquitous wireless was so much a part of the wallpaper in most homes that the boys and girls seldom talked about it. In Robin Wood the radio programmes they mentioned most often were plays, which do, in fact, demand more active co-operation from the listener than the strip magazine that is technically 'reading'. Despite all the new trends, however, the Nottingham enquirers were strongly of the opinion that those of the boys and girls who were readers (and they turned up in much the same proportion in the poor as the stylish home) were definitely among the more interesting of the boys and girls. These book readers were not pretentious about their queer taste. Indeed it made them slightly suspect, for they tended to have less common-place ideas than their friends, since their thoughts roved in worlds that were unknown to their contemporaries. The worlds were those of any adolescent reader, a jumble of poetry and science, of prehistoric animals and the hydrogen bomb, of *King Solomon's Mines* and *Kon Tiki*. Simple as their reading was, it was giving them an expanding world, and the enquirers were inclined to agree with an older friend of one of the youngsters who thought that, for all it's old fashioned to-day, there's a lot of salvation in just reading.

It was easier to get hold of the bare facts about their cinema-going than of their reading (Appendix II, Tables 5a and b). The seven days' record of 117 of the Robin Wood boys and girls showed that they had been at the pictures at least 216 times, which was a normal enough figure. The significant feature was that as many as 41 had been three or more times. Oddly enough, the Northbury figures did not give such a high proportion of intensive film-goers. The fine June weather in which the London records happened to be collected possibly had something to do with this. If they did draw a fairly typical summer-time picture of Northbury, then they indicated how very dependent upon the cinema the Nottingham youngsters had become. The comparison was the more pointed because the provincial youngsters came from solid artisan homes, were in steady jobs, had spare time in long stretches and a gamut of opportunities for a wider life.

The cinema is the traditional Aunt Sally for any Enquiry that concerns adolescents; and its balefulness almost demands a labouring of the obvious. But, for all that, this Report reiterates some of the warnings against this By-Path Meadow. In the first place the film-going of these boys and girls was of a different type from that of many of the cinema's older and more learned devotees. These youngsters mostly took their films in at least three-hour stretches, huddled into tightly rammed seats, and in a crescendo of fug and din. Secondly, since it was common for an individual to attend some two hundred or more shows in a year, they saw a great many supporting programmes which were feebler stuff on the whole than the big picture, although a large proportion of these, to judge from a bunch of titles collected at random, might be no great shakes themselves. A typical dozen that the youngsters of one area had been seeing was *Model Wife; Baby makes Three; The Assassins; Night Owls; Angel in Exile; Jungle Girl; Mister 880; Hell Fire; Kill the Umpire; Seven Days to Noon; Over the Garden Wall* and *Father is a Bachelor*. A little record of what one seventeen-year-old machinist had seen on three nights of one week—(which as a check-up showed, was quite a typical week for her) was as follows:—

PLACE AND PEOPLE

'MONDAY. This evening I went to the Waterloo, Palmer Road. I got a good seat at the price of one shilling and threepence. The film was *The Loves of Carmen*. Rita Hayworth played the colourful personality of Carmen off to perfection. Glenn Ford had the leading male role, as Don Hosea the leader of the band of gypsy highwaymen, also Carmen's husband and killer. There was some very nice Spanish dancing done by Rita Hayworth, also a thrilling knife fight between Don Hosea and Carmen's first husband. The latter gets killed. The second feature was a third rate adventure called *Hell Ship*. Also the news. And trailers. A good night's entertainment.

'WEDNESDAY. This evening I went to Tonis, Bean Road, to see *After Midnight*, starring Alan Ladd who was well up to his form as the S.S. man out to avenge the death of his best friend, caused by an unknown person who had betrayed their hide-out to the Germans. And after a lot of narrow escapes and fights, he finally tracks down the betrayer. And, as usual in films, right triumphs over wrong and the betrayer is killed. And the hero and heroine live happily ever after.

'THURSDAY. I went to Tonis again this evening, and got quite a good seat at the price of one shilling and threepence. The film was *Everybody's Cheering*, a technicolor musical. It has an amusing story, with a slight plot, considerably brightened by the brilliant dancing of Gene Kelly, and song from Frank Sinatra. I was rather disappointed that Esther Williams did not make more swimming appearances, although I don't mind saying the one she did make was lovely. The comedy was supplied by Betty Garratt and Jules Manshin. The other film was *Between Two Women*, starring Van Johnson and Gloria De Haven. It was quite good for a second feature.'

The above record has not been edited and shows that the writer was no fool. She points out, in later pages, that on the films the good girl practically always gets her man. But what she could not be expected to realize was that the situations on which her attention had been focused for the bulk of the evening were often inane if not actually anti-social. Here, so often, was the seamy side of life with a vengeance, such stuff as crimes are made of—stealing, murder (often with extreme brutality), arson, suicide, prison, drink, dope and sex-titillation. One or more of the seven deadly sins generally lay behind the title, whether this was bland or horrific. It was drama of a kind, of course, the essential material of which tales must be built. But it was not the genuine drama that would have taught her something about life. Even the film's dialogue mostly evaded the 'why' of behaviour and was no more than a connecting rod for the next bit of thrill. All told, indeed, the Nottingham enquirers came to the conclusion that even the traditional Sunday evening monkey parade, with sets of youngsters congregating in every shop entrance and corner site, might conceivably be a more civilizing process than to spend three hours (exercising neither body, tongue nor wits) in the company of the dames and guys showing at the cinema.

The thing which really troubled the interviewers was not the minutiae of the cinema's wickedness but that it represented what many of these youngsters depended on as a major source of recreation, and what a minority depended on for most of their pleasure on *several* nights of *every* week. For example, 117 of the Nottingham boys and girls affirmed that at least 216 nights of the total of 819 in the preceding week had been occupied at the pictures (Appendix II, Table 5a). On the face of it this certainly seemed undesirable. The London interviewers, to check what might have been their own prejudiced outlook, asked for the comments of the managers of various of the cinemas which the boys and girls whom they were in process of interviewing attended regularly. These managers drew attention to a different aspect of the boys' and girls' cinema-going. The first manager, a young fellow, said roughly as follows: 'It is a miserable job being a manager here and this is the toughest lot of kids in London. Our house is old and was blitzed. The directors are considering having it brought up to date in the hope that the youngsters will respect the smarter type of property. There is little or no trouble with the under-fifteens but the behaviour of the older youth is shocking. The girls are as bad as the boys, sometimes worse. They come in gangs and tear the place up. Seats are torn up, slashed with knives, and fights between rival sets are common. The type of boy has sometimes been to Borstal. During the week they come in small groups or singly and there is not much disturbance but Sunday afternoons are a nightmare. They are not much interested in what film is on, though an extra good gangster film will hold their attention.' The manager of another house, quite young himself, said:

'The behaviour here is not too bad on the whole because the management is tough and will not allow nonsense. Sunday afternoons are the worst. Girls behave better than boys at this cinema. They like plenty of action and something where they can identify themselves with the villain or the hero: no love-making for the under-sixteens and only for the girls, not the boys, over sixteen. School kids like Westerns and adventures and some comics.' The manager of a third cinema, who was an experienced middle-aged man, told this tale: 'The over-fifteens here are tough, very tough. Sunday afternoons are the bad spot of the week as they come in at four o'clock and we are not allowed to play music until the film starts. During this period they would wreck the theatre if I let them. But I've got some tough ushers and at any sign of serious trouble out the rowdies go. I've managed to establish a certain amount of control over them. It's when the film fails to hold their attention that they are so rowdy and troublesome. The girls are worse than the boys here. We have some girls whose language makes me blush—and I'm hardened. But the language of some of the women who come here gives me a shock, so you can't wonder that the kids use obscene talk as a matter of course. To my mind the youth clubs are no good—they aren't bright enough. What the youngsters want is a bit of life and the clubs are too like school. Clubs start wrong, too. Its no use trying to interest those over fifteen—they won't take it. What's needed is something for the kids of school age. Our cinema club does a lot for them. They love it and they're a good lot of little things. They're honest too. They bring me anything they find on the floor, even pennies, and they call me their "Big Chief" and we're pals. You ought to do something on a big scale for those who have to run the streets because their mothers are not at home to look after them, that's the time when they begin to get the ganging-up habit. They don't get proper meals either. I've found children—little chaps of six or seven—raking over the dustbins from the street markets and eating rotten cherries not because they're really hungry but because there's no one to look after them and see they get their tea.'

Courting, from the first tentative essays to a firm 'We're

getting engaged at Christmas', was another absorber of the free time of many of the youngsters, particularly the girls. The films and the magazines they conned so avidly spurred them on, supplying a blue print of what is expected of any young female who aspires to be reasonably attractive. Their courting, light or heavy, was taken seriously for the time being anyhow, and was not the dalliance relationship of mere dating. As a rule parents approved of the girl courting, provided she kept to certain recognized rules about it. The youngsters themselves treated it as a matter to which all other activities must give way. Some of the Nottingham boys and girls paired off as early as thirteen or fourteen. Two schoolgirls who were already much busied about boys, charged youth organizations with breaking up the romances of many of their school friends. They alleged that even the kids' gangs dissolved partly because of internal jealousies over boys. Certain of the shy and socially immature girls who at school had concentrated on their one girl crony, changed over to a similarly exclusive relationship with one boy as soon as they started work. They said they always felt left out in a crowd and were much happier to be just two. In a sense these apparently mouselike girls were not so immature, for they had begun to realize that a boy afforded a different kind of pleasure from the most trusty of female friends. Another type of early courter jumped straight from her link of school girls to 'my boy'. But she was a dashing young woman, with any amount of self-confidence and a properly competitive spirit towards rivals. She recognized the prestige that 'a boy' conferred, and she wanted to know more about the thrill-dominated process that she had heard of from older girls. It was not surprising, with all these preliminaries to courting already known to so many of the girls, that by seventeen or so serious courting was common among them. Indeed, by the time they were eighteen, some of the couples had already lived in each other's pockets for two or three years.

As far as the Nottingham boys were concerned, just a few as young as fifteen and sixteen openly admitted to having a girl friend—and the relationship seemed happy—while at least a dozen included a girl in their list of special friends. But the boys managed to have a girl friend as well as to belong to an organization, while the girls who had a serious boy, or were out to acquire one, jettisoned any idea of belonging to an organization and would do nothing in their free time that might clash with the all-important activity.

The Nottingham interviewers were in two minds about this early courting. It certainly shook sense into some of the more scatter-brained individuals, and sometimes the girl or boy friend was a provider of informal education in the more rigid sense of the word. Romance and love even at this teen-age could and did enrich some lives—noticeably so. But it aged others and it occasionally turned a girl into a wife before she had grown to be a woman. The anxiety attached to even a temporary boy weighed certain of them down, as, for example, the girl who, for all her delight in her boy and the adult status she had acquired, nevertheless admitted that courting put years on you, 'you can't be so light-hearted like'. Courting on a serious plane brought its own risks, of course. Some heartbreaking was inevitable; although apparently the most ardent affairs could crack with little frustration. On the other hand, one drowned deep in love may get bitterly hurt even at seventeen. It was not only quarrels that threatened. The call-up was a dreadful menace to those who were accustomed to spending all their free time with their boy. Less irrevocable things, for example, the boy's sudden need to attend evening classes, might also leave the girl's leisure in the lurch. She has no set of friends to fall back on, and it would not be fair to take up with a new girl friend if the relationship was only to be a stop-gap. All very difficult.

The schedule and general observation provided the above pictures as to how the boys and girls in the three areas were spending their time. And here perhaps the Nottingham enquirers may be quoted. They came to the conclusion that a considerable proportion of these youngsters, observed over a period of eighteen months, showed a negative attitude towards their leisure rather than any positive misuse of their free time. On the whole their activities were no more than spur-of-the-moment ways for curing boredom, and a repetition of last night's method of filling in, passing and killing time. There was a good deal of standing about in the street and of just strolling round the Hill. Some of the boys, even according to their contemporaries, 'mostly sat on the step', or 'went girling', or 'just hang around with a lot of lads'. Many of these nearly grown-up individuals sampled no more of the entertainment and cultural life offered by a big city than that provided by the three or four cinemas round the corner which they had been going to since they could toddle. There was seldom the question, with these near-adults, of any field of large desires. Relatively few expressed the wish to do things at all out of the ordinary, nor did most of them use their ample spending money for long-planned purchases. A good many had no creative hobby. Except for a very small minority their standard of reading was lamentable. The second rate—in films, magazines, holidays—attracted their energies to an extent which was incongruous with their education, their spending power and the amount of free time they had on hand. This indictment was certainly not true for all the boys and girls; but it held for a sufficient number to make the enquirers feel that something should be done to raise the quality of their leisure.

PART III

RELATIONSHIP WITH YOUTH ORGANIZATIONS*

WHO JOINED WHAT?

The preceding section has described how the 939 boys and girls encountered appeared to be spending their free time. It will be noticed that, up to this stage, the youth groups have hardly entered the picture. This is partly due to the fact that since the youngsters' relationship with the youth organizations was the major point of the Enquiry, the subject demanded special treatment. It also reflects the actual position, viz. that only one third of the adolescents belonged to any youth organization. 'Belonged' was interpreted somewhat differently. In London and Oxfordshire the boys' and girls' replies to the question as to whether they belonged or not related to the immediate situation. In Nottingham their answer referred to effective membership as observed by the interviewers over a period, i.e. whether the boy or girl had made a normal attendance at one or more youth organizations for part or all of a period of twenty months during the course of the Enquiry.

The main facts disclosed are as follows. Of the 939 boys and girls interviewed, 335 were members of a youth organization. In London rather more than a third were members (232 out of 643). In Nottingham, where the total adolescent population of a defined geographical area was observed over a period the proportion was much the same, i.e. one in three (44 out of 129). The combined rural areas showed a similar picture, viz. of the 167

---

* Appendix II, Table 1.

boys and girls interviewed, 59 belonged to an organization. The total membership figure for the seven urban and rural localities combined was rather over one in three.

The Enquiry showed that a larger proportion of boys than girls belonged. Nearly half the boys were members while only one in four of the girls was so. About twice as many belonged to clubs, fellowships and so on as belonged to such uniformed organizations as the Scouts and Guides, the Pre-Service units, the St. John Ambulance Brigade and the British Red Cross.

WHAT APPEARED TO AFFECT JOINING (IN THE TOWNS)*

What influenced the youngsters' joining or non-joining of organizations? Since this was the central question towards which the Enquiry was directed, particular emphasis was laid on what things, in youngster and organization, appeared to bar the two from forming a profitable relationship.

The boys' and girls' own explanations as to why they had left various societies ran something like this:

'Not interested in learning knots'	Girl Guide, 14.
'Started going out with boy'	Girls' Life Brigade girl, 15.
'It gave up'	St. John Amb. girl, 15.
'You have to go twice a week and I can't spare the time.'	Church Fellowship girl, 15.
'Packed it in when I started courting'	Club boy, 16.
'Went to work'	Club girl, 16.
'Pal left'	Club girl, 14.
'Too stuffy in the Crypt'	Club boy, 14.
'Row with leader'	Club boy, 14.
'Spiv types those of 15–19'	Club boy, 15.
'Lost interest'	Boy Scout, 14.
'Don't like map reading'	Air Training Corps boy, 15.
'Too many bosses'	Club girl, 14.
'Don't like it, don't like religion'	Club girl, 14.

* As London and Nottingham treated this subject in broadly the same way, their views are given jointly. Certain of the London views are treated more fully in 'Conclusions'. Rural Oxfordshire, so dissimilar from the two urban areas, demanded another type of approach and presented its material (summarized on pp. 96–103) somewhat differently.

'You need some time to yourself'	Army Cadet, 14.
'Didn't like the people there'	Co-op Club boy, 15.
'Too far away. Late returning'	Works Club girl, 16.
'Too much of a family clique'	Club boy, 17.
'Nobody knows what to do'	Club girl, 17.
'My friend *he* left because the boys used to pick fun out of him because he was rather thin and when he was old enough to join a higher branch of Scouts he couldn't pass the required test.'	Boy Scout, 14.
'Too many youngsters'	Club girl, 14.
'Interfered with homework'	Club boy, 15.
'Boring—you just sit there and can't get any games because the boys bag them all.'	Club girl, 15.
'Captain had favourites'	Girl Guide, 16.
'Constant changes of Scouters. Became too rowdy.'	Boy Scout, 16.
'Stopped me seeing my friends who did not belong.'	Boys' Brigade boy, 15.
'Did not care for Naval tradition'	Sea Cadet, 17.
'Enjoyed it very much but too late coming home.'	Club girl, 15.
'Not enough to do'	Club girl, 15.

One of the more common complaints of the London boys and girls was connected with their dislike of being what they called pushed around. Those from tidy homes sometimes affirmed that the groups were too rowdy for their taste. Some felt that they had got past mere youth societies, others did not know what existed. In Nottingham the boys mostly joined because they wanted to undertake some definite activity, the girls joined for company. The youngsters left the societies either for such straightforward reasons as that the group disbanded or that their friend moved house or because of personal foibles, a dislike for the Scouts' shorts perhaps, or a masculine taste or distaste for the opposite sex. Boys gave up a Club because it had, or equally had not, girls. They joined to play football and left because only the team got a game; but they just as readily left because no one there did anything *but* play football. 'Youth centre', acceptable as a title to one seventeen-year-old, suggested mere kids to a courting couple of this advanced age.

One point which teased the interviewers was whether all this that the boys and girls themselves said was of much account. The London enquirers argued that while the youngster's reasons were often highly subjective and contradicted each other, they did reflect the character of the organization to some extent and, in particular, they indicated its weaknesses. Nottingham found the whole business of leaving gluey with emotion on both sides. At the best it was tied up with a sense of uncomfortableness ('other people got on all right but I couldn't'); or guilt ('I deserted my friends and let Skip down'); or of social clash ('those girls wouldn't speak to us'). All of which was covered by the non-committal 'didn't like it'. Moreover the leader sometimes told a different tale from the member. It was he who could disclose what the boy might not choose to say, viz. that he had left in a huff because he had lost his place in the football team; or, of another boy, that he had really left because his pocket money had soared up when he changed from a factory job to one in the mines. Even leaders themselves were liable to sum up an ex-member in a variety of ways. One leader said, of a certain fourteen-year-old who had dropped out of the Scouts, that 'he was a dim, undersized, rather cheeky boy, slow witted and slow at the test work. He possibly left the troop because of his inability to compete on these lines with the other boys'. Another leader (of a Church Club) had found the boy in question 'definitely a problem type. A dreadful liar and would tell a story and then believe it himself—had to ask him to leave.' While later on a third leader (of a Pre-Service organization) said of the same youngster that he had now been with the unit for eight months and was a regular and teachable member. Moreover the most conscientious leader could do little to illuminate the leaving of those who had only nibbled at their organization. Neither the leaders' dim despondent memories, nor the other boys' vague laconicisms, revealed much about those individuals whose pencilled names, followed by three weeks' ticks and then a virgin line, trailed off at the bottom of the register of most of the youth organizations.

On the other hand it was risky to discount off-hand what the youngsters did say, as the following case suggests. Many of the Nottingham boys referred to the supposedly inferior standing of a certain club. 'They bash you up there', they muttered; or, 'You're a cissy there if you don't like boxing'; or, as several of the girls pleaded, 'My father, he won't let me go to their dances'. This all pointed to a straightforward case of social class difference until one youngster happened to mention that the Robin Wood boys seldom made their friends from those who, although they attended the same school, did not live on the side of the Parade which was covered by the Enquiry—and the club in question was on its far side. It looked as if human geography as well as social class might be involved; and that the 60-ft. wide Parade possibly still held memories of the fields which had separated two communities eighty years before. The supposition was supported by the fact that practically none of the girls of the Enquiry area joined a lively club that was quite up to their social standing and within five minutes' walk of their homes. But this club, too, was on the far side of the Parade.

PERSONALITY AND FAMILY

Although the Enquiry was a sociological and not a psychological study, the bearing of personality traits on this question of membership was too important a factor to be dismissed. At a surface level, therefore, the Nottingham interviewers did attempt some assessment. First they noticed family patterns and the impact of family attitudes on a maturing personality. Then they looked for pointers, i.e. whether the boy was at ease with his contemporaries and with people older and younger than himself, or whether he only responded to a selected group. If an 'easy' individual, did he seek out-going activities in the company of others, or was he happy in more insulated pursuits? Was the solitary hobby an expression of self-sufficiency and inner content; or was it a skilful evasion of social contacts? They noticed whether the boy was graduating through 'boys only' groups towards heterosexual ones; and whether his particular friends had interests that fostered his own potentialities. His choice of job and youth organization might indicate that he was playing for safety and running in a pattern imposed by parents. Had any grown-up, in all his sixteen years, ever offered him a close personal relationship or encouraged him to do something for somebody else? His apparent inertia might reflect the indifference of his home, or it might be a sign of his own low vitality—and so on and so forth. Physical health was another of the many possible influences on which the interviewers could make no more than a layman's comment. They did observe however that a good many of the non-members looked below par physically and had been delicate as small children and often absent from school. They noted that none of the ten Special School children they met belonged to an organization and that the rather moody, unboisterous adolescent boy who was not particularly keen on sports tended to stay on in whatever kind of society he had joined in his younger days.

While bearing the above personality and health factors in mind, the enquirers also noted how often family attitudes and the youngster's need to conform to the local social code affected his reactions to the youth groups. Indeed, if any one unshaken conclusion came out of the Nottingham Enquiry, it was that the boys and girls, although no longer real children, were still an integral part of their families. In particular they were much influenced by their elder brothers and sisters, perhaps more so than is the adolescent of the professional home. They certainly spent much of their leisure with the married brothers and sisters who, again in contrast with what generally happens in a non-artisan area, so frequently had set up their new home in or near that of the parents.

In Northbury the average number of boys and girls in a family was 3.3. A third of 177 families had five or more children, though of course not all of these were living at home. In Nottingham the majority of the families had four or more children. Two-fifths had as many as five or more; which balanced the one third which were one- or two-child families. The Nottingham enquirers wondered whether the only child joined a youth group more readily than the one with a ready-made club in the kitchen. Or, equally, did the pressure of kids stair-stepping along behind him, drive the adolescent out of the house? To judge by the small figures available neither situation seemed to make any difference. Nor did actual position in the family, whether top, bottom or middle. There was, however, some suggestion that the adolescent from the extra large household (of siblings, lodgers, in-laws and the rest) tended to belong a shade less often than the not so cumbered one.

Similar to the technically broken homes were those which had a temporarily inadequate parent, a father or mother who was an invalid perhaps, or away in gaol. One in five of the Northbury adolescents (of the 197 homes from which information was obtained on this point) had a broken home in the sense that the parents were dead or separated. The Nottingham figure (for 129 youngsters) was about one in seven. But the fact had no obvious relation with youth group membership in either area. Nor had the time honoured scapegoat of the mother being in a job, except that the more responsible of the parents in Northbury (where half of the mothers went out to work, of whom a third were in full-time jobs) were inclined to be apologetic about it. In Nottingham only 20 of the 108 mothers were in full-time employment although 32 held part-time jobs, but here again it appeared to have no bearing on the adolescents' joining or non-joining of societies.

The above aspects of the youngster's family were measurable. More elusive were the family's relationships within itself, with its immediate neighbours and with the local community. These internal relationships were a delicate matter to assess, especially since the customs relating to upbringing in the artisan home may be unfamiliar and misinterpreted by the middle-class observer. On the other hand, parents who grumbled a lot about their children to strangers, or who admitted that they came home any time, or who would not even bother to put the case for meeting the interviewers to a youngster, were probably on poorish terms with their offspring. At the other end of the scale was the excessively closely-knit home where the sixteen-year-old boy's hobbies were precisely those of his father. In Nottingham the youngsters from both types of home kept out of organizations.

It seemed plausible to expect that those from socially disinclined families would be extra prone *not* to join. Robin Wood was a cut above the arms-akimbo doorstep-chat type of district; but other pointers to neighbourliness were noticeably absent from certain of the homes. Some mothers never made friends outside their family, they didn't believe in it when you are married. Other homes had doors that were always open. Relatively few of the parents participated in activities run by the local Churches or in trade unions, or in societies for good works. Their own former membership of a youth group might have been thought to influence their attitude to to-day's units, but those who had belonged for years to the Boys' Brigade or to the Girl Guides apparently felt little allegiance to their old societies, and certainly did not push their own children into them. The family's reaction to the interviewers themselves was a relevant point. In all three areas rebuffs were experienced from prickly or indifferent families, some doubtless deserved. The Nottingham interviewers got up against two dozen of Robin Wood's hundred and fourteen households, and noted in a thriftily sociological fashion that the youngsters from these homes on the whole did not belong to societies. (It was tiresome to find that the same applied to some of those whose parents were outstandingly co-operative.) But the youngsters from the latter homes, whether in organizations or not, had a friendly attitude to people of a different age and social background and could have fitted themselves into a new group with little trouble had they wanted to. The whole situation, however, may well have been confused in Robin Wood, though less so in London and Oxfordshire, by the fact that in the old established Nottingham area so many of the families had a packet of relatives living close by. Next door cousins to shop with, the new nephew and his immaculate furnishings to display to the street, and a Grand-dad who always came to Sunday tea—these and similar pleasures almost certainly affected the need of and the time for the more formal group.

It had been thought that the family's social level* (which would still be the level of any adolescent member) might reflect itself in the type of organization the youngster did or didn't join. In examining this assumption social level was assessed on various grounds, the first of which was the father's job. The mechanical operative and the distributive trade worker were taken as the average level of employment, with the manual labourer below this and the skilled tradesman, owner-shopkeeper or clerical worker at the top of the Robin Wood tree. Secondly, the size of the house in relation to the number of occupants was assessed. And the third count on which the family's standing in the neighbourhood was measured was its housekeeping standards.

On such precarious counts as these, twenty-four families were ranked as being probably above or below the social level of Robin Wood. For what it was worth this ranking showed that two of the twelve adolescents from low level homes were effective members of a youth organization (which was below the average rate for the area), while the twelve top ranking homes had seven members which was well above the average.

EDUCATION

Another point which it was thought worth while to examine was the bearing of the youngster's formal education on his attitude to youth groups. The figures, apart from more general information collected about his schooling, gave a fairly clear picture.

About one in two of the Northbury† and the Nottingham boys who were past or present Secondary Modern School pupils belonged to a youth organization. And so did about one in three of the girls from Secondary Modern Schools in Northbury; and one in five of those in Nottingham. On the other hand, of the Grammar School boys in the urban areas, nearly three were in an

* *Elmtown's Youth.—The Impact of Social Classes on Adolescents.* Hollinshead. Wileys, New York, 1949.

† These figures for London (but not for Nottingham) include membership of evening classes and recreational evening institutes.

organization for every one who was not. The corresponding numbers for the Grammar School girls were too small to be of any significance, but of the Northbury girls who had attended a Central School three belonged for every two who did not. Although such meagre figures (concerning some 330 odd youngsters) can do no more than point to possible trends, it looked as if the more advanced his type of schooling, the more likely the adolescent was to join an out-of-school or after-work group. In Nottingham, certainly, the Grammar and the Technical School pupils spent their free time in more lively ways than the other boys and girls. Whether they were members of an organization or not, they had a wider range of things they enjoyed doing and, with much less free time and pocket money, got around more. At the same time it must be borne in mind that the difference in individuals which affected membership and behaviour may have cut across the Grammar/Modern School division.

A minor point which came out in Nottingham was that the Secondary Modern School adolescents, i.e. five of every six encountered, had had most of their full-time schooling at one or other of three schools within a very short distance of their home, a five minute saunter at most for the girls and an eight minute one for the boys. This strictly local aspect of their education (which probably holds good for the majority of city children in Secondary Modern Schools) possibly reflected itself in the geographically narrow range of their adolescent friendships, which itself may have accentuated their reluctance to face the new faces of a youth group.

Associated with the educational background of the boys and girls was the attitude of the schools themselves to youth organizations. This was somewhat delicate ground for the Enquiry to tread since its very name might suggest that it had an axe to grind. The Robin Wood Grammar and Technical Schools on the whole favoured after-school societies, provided that these had a close link with the school. In their opinion, external youth organizations, while they were desirable institutions for many youngsters, should leave the busy Grammar School scholar alone. The

Secondary Modern Schools had divergent views; some were in favour of any service that was available for their pupils, others seemed apprehensive that the amateurishness or vested interests of youth organizations might lower the standards which the school was trying so hard to set up. Whatever their private views, most of the Secondary Modern Schools had some link at official level with the local youth groups. Some did much more than this and made it their business to know what the local units were doing and which of their pupils belonged to what group. One such school had a most effective link with a club. Some of the school's staff were active members of the management committee and the club recruited regularly from the school. On the other hand an official link, or even a one-teacher link between school and youth group (a fairly constant occurrence) might be relatively ineffective as far as recruiting was concerned. What did matter was whether the school staff as a whole was so conversant with the local youth groups that the latters' activities cropped up in the daily to and fro of conversation between teachers and children. And here the difference between the schools was marked. At some schools teachers frequently spoke about the club or what they are going to do next week at the cadets; at others the children affirmed that 'We never hear anything in school about things like that'. The link did not necessarily imply that the teachers themselves were helping at the unit. Indeed, the presence of the supervising eye of a teacher might be thought to discourage membership, though it is only fair to say that, in Robin Wood anyhow, this point was never raised by the boys and girls.

Then there was the question of further education. About one in three of the Robin Wood youngsters had at some stage made some contact with an evening class though only about 23 were attending evening classes at the time when the education page of the schedule happened to be filled in. Others had been or were still going to a part-time day release course at their firm's behest. Only 6 out of 117 had actually been to an evening class according to the record they supplied of their 'last-7-days'. All told, further education (as far as day and evening classes were concerned) had touched no more than a quarter of these Nottingham boys and girls aged fourteen to seventeen. Much the same held for London. Here the overwhelming majority of those interviewed did not attend, though of course a winter survey might well have produced rather different figures. One noticeable feature in London was the number of girls who had started shorthand and typewriting on leaving school but had soon tired. The Nottingham investigation also examined the time-honoured grumble that youth groups entice away those who, at this early and vital stage of their career, should be putting their noses to the grindstone at evening classes. As might have been expected the answer was often affected by the sex of the youngster. The boys who belonged to organizations tended to have been to evening classes as well. Not so the girls although the dice were loaded for them since a Recreational Evening Institute, chiefly for women's and girls' subjects, was situated on their doorstep. Also they had a shorter working day than the boys because their jobs were nearer home.

Another point examined was how far the youngster's academic record might have affected his attitude to youth groups, since most of the latter, like school, did provide education even though it was offered in an unscholastic way. The teacher's own assessment was examined first. It was remarkable with what perspicacity a teacher's summing up of a pupil, especially in the case of the Junior Schools, had foretold the future. Most of the Robin Wood boys and girls had been ranked at school on academic as well as general grounds. The academic ranking rather suggested that the poor scholars joined organizations less than the average and high ranking adolescents—who showed about equal inclination to belong. Special aptitudes evinced at school did not seem to affect membership. The pleasure of skills practised and enjoyed there too often paled when the youngster was confronted not only with having to decide whether he really intended to work or not, but also with the difficulty of facing a new crowd of people. One exception here was those boys and girls who were really keen on games, though these tended to join a sports club rather than a youth organization as such.

The boys and girls and their parents had quite a lot to say about their own experiences of school. Much of this sounded like good sense, though some of the comment was obviously due to ignorance of the elementary purposes of education. On the whole the Robin Wood youngsters showed a lukewarm enthusiasm for their former (Secondary Modern) schools, tempered by a strong distaste in a minority of the boys and a strong liking in a minority of the girls. Real antagonism to school came more often from among the Grammar School pupils and especially from one or two of the girls who said that, among other tribulations, they had to live down the accusation that Grammar School people all think they are somebody. Their real trouble seemed to be rooted in the fact that, though they had jumped the intelligence fence easily enough, they had not managed to identify themselves with the school's social life and its predominantly middle-class flavour.

The extra year at school got much comment. The dissatisfied customer's views were most in evidence and constituted a solid block of adverse criticism. A few of the mothers who were widows or whose husbands were in low grade jobs were resentful about the year's delay in wage earning but on the whole it was not finance that the parents harped on. While they did not go so far as to say the longer schooling was mostly nonsense, they did criticize its content drastically. A joint chorus rose from parents, swelled by that of a battery of indignant aunts and uncles, that the fourteen-year-olds were 'just playing about' or 'didn't know any more' or 'never bothered to work now' or 'just did over again what they knew'. It was partly conservatism, of course, the traditional outlook that any boy as tall as his father ought not still to be fiddling about with pens and paper, and that any girl who looked a strapping wench ought to be at work. But it went deeper. It voiced a widespread feeling that school somehow was hindering the fourteen-year-old from doing the one thing that all agreed was important for him, viz. to grow up.

EMPLOYMENT

The boys' and girls' employment, as well as their education, was examined for its possible bearing on their attitude to youth organizations. As would be expected, their jobs were mostly plebeian ones. They were plumbers, painters, machinists, toolmakers, filing-clerks, packers, butcher-boys and so on. It was the exceptional boy, with a Grammar or Technical School education behind him, who was heading for a managerial post or for the professions. 'Boy' is used advisedly in this generalization, for the girls were employed in less skilled jobs and a narrower range of work than their brothers. In both London and Nottingham the typical girl was the one who did a routine manual job in a factory. Even in Northbury, for all its nearness to the City, few of the girls had clerical jobs; nor did many of the Robin Wood girls go into office or even shop work. About half the Nottingham girls were mechanical operatives, and many of them were machinists and cutters in the hosiery trade. They were definitely 'work girls' rather than factory girls, however; and their job carried none of the stigma that Central London still attaches to the latter term. Incidentally, not one of them was in work which gave her any training for running a home or raising children.

The wages of the Robin Wood adolescents appeared to be round about the £3 level, if one figure is taken for the youngsters as a whole. The miner and the quick-fingered over-locker who was prepared to work hard might earn £5 or over, while the apprentices, shop girls and routine clerical workers received perhaps not more than 45s. a week. Three features of their earning power were much in evidence. *Firstly* these juniors were well aware that unless they were grossly incompetent their wages would increase automatically and frequently*: so that as regards money they had not much incentive to make a particularly good job of their work. This increase was not necessarily a steady one, as is shown by the following figures, taken from one girl's actual pay packets which she had preserved. At fifteen she earned 43s.; at fifteen and a half 96s., 102s., 64s., 46s., 84s., 90s., 85s.; at sixteen, 82s., 76s., 77s., 90s., 140s., 121s.; and at sixteen and a half, 91s., 70s., 108s. On the other hand some of the girls were put

*Appendix II, Table 5c.

onto piece work only a few weeks after they had left school, which, of course, challenged them to work energetically, although it was not, perhaps, a very sound introduction to 'work' regarded as a career. *Secondly,* even the older adolescents did not have full control over their wages. Most of the girls and many of the boys did not yet pay their board at home. Until they were about eighteen (and therefore beyond the age of most of the adolescents with whom the Enquiry was concerned) they handed their regular wage, less the week's pocket money and less any bonus or overtime pay, to their mother, and looked to the latter to provide their clothes, shoe repairs, holidays, meals out, fares and in some cases even such things as cigarettes and lipsticks. Whatever cash they handled themselves each week was money to burn, so to speak, and was expected to go on personal pleasures. Nor did the money they gave into their home relate at all closely to what they earned. The 25*s.* they gave in at sixteen might perhaps have risen to 30*s.* at seventeen; but more often than not the original contribution was unchanged—and it was just too bad for Mum. London customs were different. The new wage earner tended to go 'on board' quite soon after he left school so he learnt to do most of his own essential spending at an earlier age than did his contemporaries in the provinces. Many of the London parents did not seem to direct their children's spending at all, so it naturally went on immediate satisfactions, on entertainment, cosmetics, cigarettes, ice cream, the latest in personal knick-knacks, and so on. The majority of the Camdington girls who were interviewed said that if they were earning more they would use it for clothes. They often bought these through a club. If they had a boy friend, and marriage was not too far ahead, they might perhaps save a bit; and they were prepared to work overtime for some months before the wedding. And *thirdly* it was noticeable that practically all the youngsters in both London and Nottingham appeared to have ample money for spur-of-the-moment purchases, although the Londoners were often spent out by the middle of the week. In Robin Wood too, if money beyond their own income could buy the things they yearned after, they generally, with the family's help, got them.

Their wages had, of course, to be considered in the light of any technical training they were receiving from their employer. About one in three of the Robin Wood youngsters had had some definite training. The others, by their own account, just did what they were shown or watched others until they knew the ropes. The change over from school did not appear to worry them, even though their working hours were so much longer than those at school. In Nottingham conditions were noticeably good. The absence of heavy machinery and metallic goods and the prevalence of soft materials like clothes and tobacco and toilet goods meant clean and not too clanking workrooms. Indeed the Robin Wood youngsters often praised their firm's attention to welfare. About half of them had a 44-hour week or even shorter and only a fifth (21 out of 103) received less than two weeks annual paid holiday—which was a happy and glorious improvement on the picture that the interviewers would have found ten years earlier. Indeed, it compared well with the London conditions where a considerable number of these young boys and girls still had no more than one week's holiday in the year.

Both in London and in Nottingham the boys and girls, on the whole, expected their jobs to be near at hand. In Robin Wood as many as one in three got home to their mid-day meal. The strictly local job tended to confine their life at an age when a wider physical world would have been an education in itself. It may even have helped to explain their diffidence about venturing into the new world of a youth group. In London it was noticed that the more advanced the youngster's job the more he tended to belong to some organization. The Post Office employees (carefully selected and in a paternal organization), boys who were with printers and bookbinders, and those working in the furniture and carpentry trades, mostly belonged to some youth group, while the van and errand boys did not. It was the same in Robin Wood. Those whose type of job was below the average were rather less likely to belong than the apprentices and trainees. On the other hand boys in the really skilled jobs did not make particular use of youth groups. As for the girls, few of those in the lower level factory jobs of either London or Nottingham belonged to an organization. Over-frequent change of jobs was not a very marked feature of either area though any figures must of course be related to the age structure of those concerned (Appendix II, Table 1). In Robin Wood, for example, only about one in seven of the adolescents had had more than three jobs. More than half were still with the firm at which they had started. In London the choice of first job was definitely felt by the parents to be their responsibility; but once the youngster had embarked on the adult world of work he was expected thence-forward to look after himself. Perhaps this traditional outlook, together with memories of the depression, helped to explain why the Youth Employment Service in Central London got less support than its conscientious work certainly justified.

A point that provided more food for thought than the kaleidoscopic career-story of the few was the attitude of the more sensible youngsters to their jobs. In London it was clear that many of the parents were still too near to the bad old days themselves for them to look on their child's work as more than what brings in this week's food and clothes. Robin Wood had fewer unhappy memories, and the parents took a good deal of care as to the conditions under which their child worked, although they often had limited notions about any real career for him or, more particularly, for her. What seemed very significant about 'work' was that while some of the youngsters were obviously working very hard, a good many appeared to be ambling through their day's job. This was particularly noticeable among the girls. In the first place they were less ambitious than the boys, less proud of their tools, less prepared to sacrifice their spare time to classes, less ready to put up with lower wages for the sake of learning a trade. Even the ex-Grammar school girls did not speak of their jobs as did the boys, who talked cheerfully of having a lot to learn yet and were often willing to accept a relatively low wage for the sake of their training. Moreover the girls had no call-up, the mere expectation of which widened the outlook of many of the boys.

If the latter were dissatisfied with their present job they spied new possibilities via the training schemes of the Services. On the other hand a girl such as a cycle assembler or an aspirin packer or the back girl on a lace pantograph machine, could become reasonably proficient at her job in a few months. Some of them, especially those who had been in the 'C' stream at school, were content with a simple job like folding cartons or magnetizing cycle hubs, 'a thousand a day or two thousand if you feel like it'. Even the brighter ones were often happy enough in the routine job for the first year or so, since novelty, plus three pound notes next Friday, put a halo round the dullest job. But the glamour dimmed in time; and though few actually put their trouble into words, glimpses of it showed among the older ones. The incentive of a big wage later on did not often act as a spur even to the more able girls, because they believed, whatever the facts, that after they were about twenty-one they would not be able to make much increase in their earnings. Others, career-minded rather than money-minded, complained that they had 'only been to that school so what else could we have started on but office or factory or shop?' Their grumble may have been true, and the school may never have suggested anything beyond the kind of work which is traditional in Robin Wood, but the really distressing thing was that they believed they were too old (at seventeen) to start on a new type of work.

It was noticeable how often the girls were held back by one fact, viz. that their artisan world had not yet compromised on the marriage or career question. By the time they reached seventeen or so, probably most of these girls were expected to have come down on one side or other of this fence. The responsible ones and the born mothers, perhaps the majority, found it their duty as well as their pleasure to plump for a future in which all their energy would go on what they described as 'being a Mum'. Just one or two of the more thoughtful ones had a feeling and a conscience that even a girl's job might be one which, as they said, 'would do something that mattered for the world.' They and the career-minded girls were of course human enough, although their friends regarded them as odd fish, to want to marry eventually. But the whole business was a worry to them; and there seemed a strong case for presenting the alternative of marriage or career in not quite such black and white terms. In a sense these particular girls were pioneers in their own social world and they ought not to have had to limit themselves for fear that, if they stood out for a career rather than just a job, they would be disloyal to their own femininity. It was not merely a question of their present peace of mind, although, if right with their job, they were likely to be right with the world generally. Their contentment in later life might well be bound up with their ability at that stage to pick up their original career, as distinct from just going out to work. Career or no, these adolescent girls of the 1950's were heading for a future in which they would almost certainly spend a smaller proportion of a longer life in child-raising than their mothers did.

'MY FRIENDS'

The last, and one of the most difficult subjects which the enquirers examined in relation to the youngster's joining of societies, was his particular set of friends. 'See you tomorrow night,' the parting words of any of the small sets of adolescents observed, suggested that their friends played an even more important role in the life of these youngsters of fourteen to seventeen than had the children's gangs of their younger days. The school children's cliques, to judge by the examples current in Robin Wood, sprang from what might be called compulsive propinquity. They were highly local affairs, with strict territorial limits and doubtless rigid rules of entry and dismissal. Some of them had no permanent helmsman; but in general one person was in command, even if only temporarily. The set might take its name from him. He was more often the group's tough guy than its 'idea-merchant', but what he commanded was done. The character of the sets varied; and they were often in rivalry with each other. For example the Rookery (a district name) gang beat other children up, and schoolgirls said they daren't go down there. The sets were alleged to operate during the week rather than on Saturdays and Sundays when the grown-ups were about. They were seasonal, too, in that cliques which had thriven in the long dark evenings might disappear when the summer came. The children pointed out the advantages of belonging to one set or other. Brute force being a genuine menace when you are nine or ten, you are likely to suffer physically if you do not belong to some group. Moreover in a bunch you feel big and you impress the girls better. In other words these street cliques were not only fun but also a safety measure. They were sometimes a compensation as well, for the more the child's home was one that gave him a scanty welcome indoors, the more he tended to rely on his friends outside.

As they got older the youngsters graduated from a tangle of children (knotted through the proximity of their yards and houses) into smaller, more selective groups. They began to choose their friends for specific reasons, though they generally retained at least one of the original set—often a child whom they had played with since they were tiny. Indeed the long standing of many of their adolescent friendships was remarkable. It was noticeable, too, that they used the term 'my friend' less loosely than did younger children or grown-ups. 'My friend' implied a special relationship for them; and they knew precisely what names to write down when asked if they would say on the schedule a little about their particular cronies. They often included a brother or sister in their list; and the large size of so many of their families doubtless afforded a useful variety of combinations among siblings. At least a third of the Robin Wood girls had a particular friend of the opposite sex, and a sixth of the boys included a girl among their special friends. Most of their lists were quite short (three-quarters of the youngsters gave three or less names), while for certain of the girls it was no more than 'just me and her' or 'only my boy and me'. In general the boys had no longer a list of special friends than the girls. On the whole these little adolescent sets were more closely knit than the children's, for all they were subject to violent upheavals. Some youngsters spent a vast amount of their free time (and sometimes their working time too) with their particular friends, and they fraternized relatively little with other contemporaries. They met according to most regular patterns. A fifteen-year-old shop girl who listed two girls and five boys as 'My friends' saw No. 1 girl every night, No. 2 girl and No. 6 boy on Thursdays and Sundays, and the rest on Mondays, Thursdays and Sundays. It was as neat as that.

Sometimes a set of friends could be identified as the idle but vigilant little group which haunted a particular spot, a corner doorway, or a juke-drenched milk bar. By about seven o'clock one or two of them were practically always on the known spot; and the others could be guaranteed to turn up, descending like a whirlwind more often than not, on their ramshorn-handlebarred bikes. Or the set met regularly at each others' homes, on the night when the grown-ups were always out. It was a pleasant feature of Robin Wood to come across several girls toasting themselves before the fire in a gossipy way; or to find a trio of boys having an evening with the gramophone. One big set, of a rather different kind, had been in existence for years although its constituents had changed. This was a group of about two dozen boys who played football together on Sunday mornings on the Hill. There was a bit of rough usage perhaps; but on the whole the game was satisfactory, and it was an important part of the lives of these particular boys. The leading spirits were two or three boys who did not seem to be in any youth organization.

The assets of the close set of friends were obvious. As the youngsters so touchingly affirmed, these were pals whom time could not alter. At that age, too, they might well prove to be the ones from whom life's most significant friend would eventually emerge. For the time being, anyhow, these friends provided dependable company and, on occasion, financial aid; they supported each other in the inevitable growing pains of the break with home; and they were people with whom to discuss all the important and fascinating things that musn't be mentioned elsewhere. Above all, the values and the jokes of these pals were one's own, so that in such company even the very shy felt at ease.

It was plain that the youngster's set of friends directly affected his relationship with the larger more formal group of a youth organization. Compared with the length and strength of their allegiance to their friends most of the Robin Wood boys' and girls' dealings with the youth organizations had had as precarious a life as an autumn leaf. Moreover the strength of these ties and the robustly independent social life that some of them engendered, made the Nottingham interviewers wary of intrusion. They felt that, except in the case of any notorious gang, there should be no question of asking youngsters to show old friends the door, in any effort to get the youngster into an organization. What an organization should try to do was to build on existing allegiances and offer the little private group more scope. And any salesmanship for the youth organization should be directed not just at one youngster but at his buddy and 'My friends.'

The enquirers also confirmed what is a commonplace, viz. that on the whole the normal adolescent makes his special friends from people of roughly his own age or, in the case of the girl, with a boy rather older than herself. Among the Robin Wood youngsters only the most dreary individual, or the one who was held locally to be a bit weak in the head, included anyone much younger than himself in his own particular set. This point came into prominence when the age structure of the Robin Wood youth organizations was analysed and it was found that their membership was weighted on the side of those aged fifteen and under (Appendix II, Table 4). As the figures showed, any adolescent as old as sixteen and seventeen who was looking casually as the local youth organizations, would have seen them as groups more juvenile than himself and not, therefore, as people from whom he would normally make his particular friends.

NATURE OF THE YOUTH ORGANIZATIONS IN NOTTINGHAM

Up to this point the Report has concerned itself with the background and habits of the boys and girls themselves. But since joining any society is a two-way affair, the youth organizations as well as their potential members demanded at least a cursory examination.

RELATIONSHIP WITH YOUTH ORGANIZATIONS 91

To take Nottingham. Most of the organizations encountered were very conscious of being a part of the Youth Service of their city, and proud that Nottingham had so long a tradition of caring for its young people. The leaders recalled that in the depression of the 1930's (which was the time when the older adolescents of the Enquiry were being born) the Nottinghamshire Miners' Federation and the National Association of Boys' Clubs undertook a pioneer work in setting up clubs for young miners. Moreover, since 1943 the University has provided a course in youth leadership. This meant that, at the date of the Enquiry, fifteen students were making regular contact with certain of the city's youth groups as part of their training. During the war, too, Nottingham obtained a detailed analysis of its youth work;* and it is an interesting little reflection that the youngsters of that wartime survey were the elder brothers and sisters whose example was so often quoted to the enquirers by the current adolescent population.

In 1949 the city's Youth Committee estimated that about two-fifths of its population aged fifteen to twenty belonged to youth organizations. Two hundred and eighty-seven youth units were actually registered with the Authority. The latter spent about £18,000 annually on its Youth Service, paid the salary of twenty-four full-time leaders and on the whole was considered to be generous in its provisions of instructors, equipment and playing fields.

At the time of the Enquiry thirty-six organizations open to those of adolescent age were within an easy walk of the Robin Wood Enquiry area. Eighteen were units that wore some kind of uniform, the other eighteen were clubs (see Appendix II, Table 4a). They were under the aegis of an assortment of adult bodies, the Local Education Authority, the schools, the Churches, the Co-operative Society, etc.; and between them they were affiliated to most of the major national voluntary youth organizations. About 180 grown-up people helped regularly at the above organiza-

* *Youth Service in an English County.* L. J. Barnes. King George's Jubilee Trust, 1945.

tions (the great majority being of course voluntary). Twenty-five part-time instructors and pianists were paid by the Local Authority who also provided part of the salary of six of the leaders. In spite of this relatively high proportion of professional leaders, nearly all the units were understaffed, and a number of them which had the facilities to expand were held back by lack of helpers. Such children's societies as the Brownies, Life Boys, and so on, fed these adolescent groups, and, to a much lesser extent, the latter passed on their older members to adult societies. The typical size of the unit was round about 30 to 40 youngsters, though as many as one in five had over 100 members. The typical unit held one or two meetings a week, and the typical subscription was 3*d*. or less. One point about these adolescent groups which has already been referred to, was that they were slightly weighted on the side of those aged under fifteen. In other words about five of the members were at school for every four at work.

The units were well housed. Four of the clubs had the use of buildings that really looked as if they were planned for young people and were moreover warm, well lighted and pleasantly decorated. They had such things as a stage, halls for badminton and dancing, rooms for metal and woodwork and plenty of space for billiards and indoor games. Some of the groups, of course, had to make do with bare and benchy Church halls or with school classrooms that were brightly juvenile. But they were in a minority. Even the less functional premises at least had a cared-for look. Facilities for outdoor games, too, were relatively good. Football pitches were not impossibly scarce, nor too far away; while the Education Committee allowed any recognized group to use the tennis courts and netball pitches of a Grammar School that was just off the area. There was always room on the Hill for the rounders type of game and a swimming bath was within ten minutes' walk.

Programmes also were of a good standard. Those of the uniformed organizations were typical and were undertaken in an alert way, while those of the clubs were mostly of the kind (and a good kind at that) which provided drama, P.T., table-tennis, boxing, crafts, dancing, concerts and discussion groups. A number of the units ran week-end camps throughout the year; and as many as two in three troubled to fix up a holiday party, to the Isle of Wight, to North Wales, to Devon and to other rather more adventurous spots than the traditional 'Skeggy or Mablethorpe' of the East Midlands. About two in three of the groups had their own youngsters' committee, Court of Honour or similar institution, which, in the majority of cases, was more than a mere bow to democracy. One great asset that most of the Robin Wood organizations possessed was that so many of them had been in the field for a relatively long time. Only seven were post-war infants.

There were inevitable exceptions to this somewhat rosy and generalized picture. At certain of the organizations the members were bored and therefore rowdy. Some of the adult helpers were the kind of people who, according to the youngsters, said the unit would do this and that but it never did. There was also a good deal of slipshod record keeping. But on the whole the thirty-six units within a few minutes' walk of the boys and girls were numerous, varied, decently housed, well-rooted and judged to be quite up to the level of youth work in other parts of the country. Why nearly two-thirds of the local adolescents made no effective contact with them during the eighteen months of the Enquiry did not appear to be primarily due to any inefficiency in the units' leaders, premises, constitutions, or programmes. However, certain other reasons for the youngsters' attitude did come to the surface during the investigators' contact with the area.

In the first place, as far as could be ascertained without specific enquiry, not more than three or four of the two thousand adults living actually within the Enquiry area (and the immediate neighbours, therefore, of the boys and girls) held any responsibility for the above three dozen units. Thus, none of the two hundred or so parents of the youngsters had any regular contact with the local youth groups, nor, apparently, with groups elsewhere. In other words, these families bringing up adolescents had no link at adult level with the organizations set up specifically for the welfare of their children. The situation was normal enough; and fifty years ago it would probably have been inevitable. But the point is that people and times—leisure times in particular—have changed. People have more time and money nowadays to spend on things other than the needs of their own home; and they are perhaps more alive to the fact that adolescents have their own particular needs and problems. It was encouraging to see how many of the local adults took a keen interest in particular youngsters whom they had watched grow up, and expressed a genuine concern for certain of the under-privileged boys and girls. This concern was not a generalized one. The adults did not think in terms of character training or citizenship. What they noted was young Freddie Smith 'wasting his five pounds a week on trash'; and the Robinson girl 'sixteen and never going out except with her mother'. Nor did they think in terms of Service. Indeed they were over-modest about their capabilities. But the essential goodwill was there, as doubtless it had been in their grandparents' days when churches and trade unions would perhaps have harnessed it more often than they do to-day.

It boiled down to this. Most of the organizations needed additional help; and many of the local adults were potential helpers on a small scale, that is, they could have given a limited amount of time to what might sound like small and insignificant jobs. As things were, however, the youth groups made so slight an impact on the adults living in their vicinity that the latter seldom felt any responsibility towards them and were quite unaware that their help would have been appreciated. Even the adults who had adolescent children themselves, though they knew roughly what units existed, knew very little about the adults who ran them nor, in any detail, what went on there. And they certainly had no conception of the youth groups' ultimate aims. The curious point was that this held not only for the low-level inarticulate home, which did not reckon to direct anyone as old as an adolescent, but it also applied to those which were very much alive to the needs of their younger members. Most of these more intelligent parents regarded the local organizations as a vaguely good thing but only in the negative sense of keeping youngsters off the streets. In other words though these youth organizations had, since 1939, grown into a joint association of statutory and voluntary bodies, the enterprise still lacked a third and vital partnership, that of the parents of the adolescents themselves.

PART IV

THE ENQUIRY IN THE COUNTRY AREAS

OXFORDSHIRE AND BUCKS*

THE ABOVE observations have dealt with the situation as found in the urban area of Nottingham and, to a lesser extent, in London. A more detailed analysis of the Northbury and Camdington organizations is given in 'Conclusions'. The Oxfordshire villages provided a very different picture and, as has been said before, the material relating to them was dealt with in a rather different way from that of the other two areas.

Four villages were concerned, three in Oxfordshire and one in Buckinghamshire, all within a thirty-mile radius of the City of Oxford. The first of these was 'Melbury', a small community of about 250 people. It is an isolated place eight miles from a railway station. The second village was 'Chadlicott', a larger place with a population of 750. The latter is near enough to a market town for this to provide a weekly exodus for the villagers, while Oxford itself is only fifteen miles away. The other two places, 'Mersham' and 'Upper Hinton', are large by English village standards, since each has a population of about 2,000. They, too, are near enough to urban centres for this to influence their economic and social life. Many Mersham people travel the $3\frac{1}{2}$ miles to Oxford for their work, while Upper Hinton is almost contiguous with the outskirts of a town and in many respects its life is linked with that of the town.

Melbury is situated in a very rural area in the north west of the county, and agriculture is the main occupation. The farms are

* Prefatory Note and Appendix II, Table 1.

mixed and not necessarily owned by local people. It is a sandstone and thatch village, dipping from the Church, which stands high at the top of the village street, down to a stream. It also has a Methodist Chapel; but neither parson nor minister live in the village. The school was closed in 1947. Its premises are available for meetings and the county library functions there once a week. At the time of the Enquiry the village had only eleven adolescents and there were no organizations for them or for the younger children. One boy and one girl were members of organizations outside Melbury, and most of the boys belonged to a cricket club in a neighbouring village.

Chadlicott is a rather more prosperous and attractive looking place. It has a Manor House, several other large houses and substantial farms. Situated fairly high, it stands in an undulating landscape of parks and woodland. Although near enough to two centres of population for these to provide a variety of employment and services—shops, secondary schools, cinemas, etc.—it is large enough to engender a social life of its own. As in Melbury there is an Anglican and a Free Church, but unlike Melbury the vicar here lives in the village. It has a Junior School, a sizeable village hall, a playing field and tennis courts. When the Enquiry was being made its societies included a Women's Institute and, for the younger generation, there was a Boys' Brigade and a Girl Guide Company. Fourteen boys and ten girls aged fourteen to seventeen were interviewed: and of those, five boys and five girls belonged to youth organizations, though not all of these societies were situated in Chadlicott itself. In contrast with the stereotyped pursuits of the London and Nottingham youngsters, the boys and girls of these two villages produced relatively varied programmes. They mentioned reading (though in one village only two of the ten used the County Library), cycling, swimming, cricket, football and table tennis as well, of course, as the radio. The boys went for walks, shot rabbits, gardened and kept pets. The girls had a good many domestic duties. Figures for the twenty-four boys and girls showed that most of them had been to the cinema in the last seven days, four of them twice, and one

G

of them three times. Cycling, walks and swimming had occupied sixteen of the boys and girls and practically all of them had watched or played cricket. Seven of the girls recorded some housework.

Mersham's history dates back to Saxon times but for all its former fame and its nearness to Oxford it is a quiet and little known village. A certain number of the people are employed on the land, others work in the motor industry at Cowley and in the blanket trade and other light industries of Witney. The village itself is big enough to provide employment in its own shops, inns, garages, builder's yards and so on. Many of the Mersham homes are old and very small; but there are a few larger houses on the outskirts and a considerable number of both pre- and post-war council houses. The village has an Anglican and a Roman Catholic Church, both with a resident incumbent, and a Baptist Chapel served by a visiting minister. It has a joint Primary and Secondary Modern School. The Headmaster, who in 1951 was trying to make the school a centre for educational opportunities, had organized a variety of evening classes.

Mersham's adult societies at the time of the Enquiry included a Women's Institute and a British Legion. One of the more indigenous groups was a Concert Party which had been built up during the past three years, largely through the enthusiasm of a local teacher. Its programme ranged from popular songs and drama of the variety type to country dancing. The latter included a traditional dance of the old Mersham Mummers, accompanied by recorders. Most of the Concert Party were adolescents and so were the members of the Table Tennis Club. Young people were also catered for by a Scout Troop and by an Air Training Corps, founded in 1949. The latter met twice a week in a disused Royal Air Force hut, The cadets could use these premises for informal activities on other evenings if they so wished. From 1943 to 1948 the National Association of Boys' Clubs had had an affiliated club in Mersham, with a membership of about thirty-five boys. But it had functioned intermittently and in 1951 the sole off-shoot was a football club. The question of more adequate provision for

Mersham's young people had exercised the village for some years, and it had set up a Committee to acquire a site and draw up plans for a Youth Centre. A start had been made on the foundations but the work was being held up for lack of materials and labour.

The physical appearance of the boys' and girls' homes in Mersham showed a good deal of variety. Some were well kept and provided a cultural and moral background that fortified the school's efforts. Others did not. The youngsters had plenty of ideas about new recreations which they would like to try. Moreover they knew a good deal about the youth organizations of other places, and were very anxious to get a good club going in Mersham. Sixty-two adolescents, twenty-six boys and thirty-six girls were interviewed. Their total membership of societies (which included those who belonged to more than one) showed that thirteen boys and two girls were members of adolescent youth organizations, twelve boys and girls were in children's groups and six boys and eighteen girls belonged to one or other of the adult societies.

Upper Hinton, the last of the four villages and the one in Buckinghamshire, is situated on a chalk ridge of the Chilterns, three and a half miles from a town. Its altitude, its lack of a natural water supply and the difficulties of communication had kept it isolated up to about 1930, when London Transport arrived and considerably modified the structure and the habits of the population. At the date of the Enquiry, although the public services in Upper Hinton were of a higher standard than that of many villages of its size, not all the cottages had electricity or piped water. It had other omissions, no resident doctor, no nurse and no incumbent. Indeed until sixty years ago the village possessed no Church, though it had been more favoured as regards education. Its Dame School had been succeeded first by a Church School and then by a Primary and Secondary Modern School. The Secondary School has several acres of grounds and is well known for its work in rural education. It also has a high standard in handiwork, which the staff attributes partly to the long tradition of craftsmanship in the Chilterns.

Upper Hinton's major industry still derives from the surrounding beechwoods. Although the big furniture manufacturing firms are highly mechanized, the small ones, which make such things as chair legs and tennis racquets, even today rely on hand worked lathes and other simple machines. Cottage industries for women have also survived to a surprising extent. Many families undertake tambour work and rouleau and make ornamental buttons and fringes for the London and Paris houses, whose agents distribute the materials and collect the finished goods. In addition to its own local types of work the village has a small clothing factory, while its nearness to a town provides many varieties of employment.

Most of the Upper Hinton homes that the interviewer visited had a high standard of housekeeping and the cared-for look of the young people was noticeable. Few appeared under-nourished, poorly dressed or in any way neglected and very little real poverty was evident. The village had a vigorous social life. The Churches were much in evidence. Anglican, Baptist and Methodist each had its Sunday School and almost every child in the village had attended one or other. Some of the older boys and girls belonged to choirs and in particular to two Methodist Guilds. The Senior one held weekly meetings and had an attendance of forty to sixty. At the Baptist Church there was a Children's Sunshine Corner, a weekly meeting for mothers, and, a somewhat unusual feature, a Women's Fellowship for those of any denomination. Besides weekly meetings, the Churches organized many *ad hoc* events; and they united for such occasions as Empire Youth Sunday and Armistice Day. The secular groups ranged from the Village Hall Committee which was raising funds for new premises, to the Village Produce Association, which held an annual show and gave practical advice to beekeepers, fruit growers and so on. The British Legion, a robust body with both a men's and women's group, possessed its own hall and presided over many village functions. Then there were the sports societies. The Cricket Club had a couple of teams. It had no age limit, and no subscription, as its funds were raised through collections made at the Saturday afternoon matches on the Common. The players' wives provided the tea and once a year they and the Club held a dinner in the Legion Hall. The Football Club had as many as three teams, one a minor, and all in a League. It provided its own trainer and had its own Supporters' Club which arranged dances and outings. A good many of the adolescents belonged to this. On the whole Upper Hinton supported its societies and its many dances and socials pretty well; and some people had few winter evenings free from one function or another.

The above activities were primarily for adults. The national voluntary youth organizations are stronger in the county of Buckinghamshire than in Oxfordshire but few had units within reasonable distance of Upper Hinton. The village itself had a mixed Youth Club with about thirty members aged fourteen to eighteen, a pack of Brownies, a Guide Company, and a Junior Red Cross which children of twelve could join. The Club met in what had been the Church School. Here it had two fair-sized halls, an office and a small kitchen-cum-canteen. One hall had a stage, the other had tables for snooker and table tennis. A Junior section of this club was open to boys and girls aged twelve to fourteen and a half and met three times a week. The annual subscription was 1s 6d. to 5s. (according to age) and the nightly one was 3d. The Club was run by a full-time leader, voluntary helpers and a committee of three girls and two boys which held fortnightly meetings. The Senior club had an interesting and varied programme. Two of its table tennis teams were in a league and each had its own captain, secretary and committee. There were also netball, cricket, and lawn tennis groups, all of which were sufficiently advanced to play matches. The Club took in various magazines, had its own library, a branch of the county library, and ran a German class. Two of its activities were held in conjunction with a Club in the neighbouring village. One was a weekly class in play production, and the other a monthly Olde Tyme Dance. This latter included the services of a professional instructor and the loan of gramophone records, all for 6d.

Seventy of the Upper Hinton boys and girls, aged fourteen to seventeen were interviewed. Their total membership (which included those who belonged to more than one society) showed that nineteen boys and fifteen girls were in adolescents' organizations, nineteen were in children's societies and fifteen boys and the same number of girls belonged to organizations that were primarily for adults. A higher proportion of the Upper Hinton youngsters belonged to a society of one kind or another than did those in Mersham, and only fifteen were not in any formal group. But then, more organizations existed in Upper Hinton.

The adolescents displayed considerable differences in the two villages of Mersham and Upper Hinton in the imagination and initiative with which they used their leisure. In Mersham, a place where most of the adults' social activities did not readily flourish, the youngsters had many ideas on what they would have liked but were unable to do. The Upper Hinton youngsters tended to belong to the adult organizations of their village. The Mersham boys and girls went to towns and to the pictures more often than those from Upper Hinton. They also gave more evidence of boredom and frustration and had occasional bouts of actual delinquency. On the whole, however, the passive entertainment of the town did not play a large part in the lives of any of these country-bred youngsters. It increased the nearer they were to a town, the easier their transport facilities, and the more their jobs were urban ones. The cinema played an important part in the leisure of those youngsters who were courting since it was the accepted way of entertaining a friend of the opposite sex.

In both villages the boys and girls criticized the youth organizations on, broadly, the following grounds. Certain of the boys found the discipline in some organizations too authoritative, others were bored by the activities provided. Boys left adult games clubs because they found they did not get enough games. Some of the girls complained that at a particular organization no one there paid them any attention. In another group, although individual girls did not mention it, the average age showed it was really geared to younger children. By the statements which a number of girls made about their ideal club, and the reasons given for leaving or for not joining one of the organizations which met in noticeably poor premises, it was clear that to these girls a poor physical standard was one reason for their lack of support. At another organization the meeting time for those who worked in the neighbouring town was too early. Home responsibilities was another reason for not belonging to any youth organization. The summing up seemed to be that the children's organizations were really too juvenile for those in their teens, while the adult ones made too few concessions to adolescent tastes and usage. In Upper Hinton the Youth Club was meant to fill this gap, and to some extent it did; but it was not entirely adequate for the boys, and it failed markedly as far as the girls were concerned.

PART V

CONCLUSIONS

CONCLUSIONS RELATING TO THE BOYS AND GIRLS

THE ENQUIRERS found that their conclusions fell into two categories. The first category related to the immediate issue, viz. why a larger proportion of the nine hundred and thirty-nine boys and girls met did not think it worth their while to join any of the organizations set up specifically for the enjoyment and welfare of the adolescents of their neighbourhood. The second category concerned the general well-being of the boys and girls, particularly in so far as this was affected by the way in which they spent their free time.

As regards the first issue, while it was relatively plain sailing to determine who was or was not an effective member at any set time, further investigation often revealed that a contradictory reply would have been received had the question been asked on a different date. At such an essentially fluid stage as adolescence, the 'joiner' or the 'non-joiner' label can only be tied on loosely; and the interviewers could not elicit any one answer to their perennial queries—'Why did you join; why didn't you join; why did you leave such and such an organization?' Neither the study of individuals over a period (as was undertaken in Nottingham), nor observation plus statistical analysis on a small scale (as was used in London and Oxfordshire) suggested that there existed an all-embracing answer to this question. One of the seventeen-year-old girls possibly put her finger on a significant point when she said that a good many of her contemporaries were almost incapable of joining an organization because it would necessitate too great a change in their established way of life.

CONCLUSIONS

Such a difficulty as the above is inherent in the personality and social habits of the youngster himself, which is only half the story. The youth groups for their part, as they were only too ready to admit, had their own limitations. These were more often related to inadequate personal relations than to faulty administration or to moribund programmes. The one firm conclusion that did emerge was that to become an effective member of a formal group is a more complicated business for the adolescent than is generally assumed. An uncommon amount of good-will and of horse-sense is essential on both sides to produce the active member and the influential society. In other words the boy or girl who is an effective member of a youth group has indeed accomplished something.

How many had reached this stage? In round figures one in three of these boys and girls aged fourteen to seventeen belonged to youth organizations (232 out of 643 in London, 44 out of 129 in Nottingham, and 59 out of 167 in the villages). In London about three and in Nottingham about two boys belonged for every girl. Approximately twice as many belonged to clubs, fellowships and so on as to such uniformed organizations as Scouts and Guides, the Pre-Service units, the St. John Ambulance Brigade and the British Red Cross.

Although only about a third of these adolescent boys and girls were members, the great majority had belonged to one society or another when they were children or, more specifically, before they were fourteen. This held for both the rural and the urban areas. In Mersham and Upper Hinton 119 out of 132 adolescents had been in a juvenile group like the Brownies or Sunday School; while in Robin Wood as many as 106 had at some stage been members of one of the recognized weekday organizations for children. It was established therefore that the majority of the adolescents had had some first-hand experience of what it is like to be a voluntary member of a society.

It was also established that in all three areas the break with their children's societies tended to occur about the age of fourteen. Nottingham found that while 39 out of 100 adolescents had left some kind of organizations before they were fourteen, only sixteen had left at an older age. In London about two-thirds (258 out of 374) of those who had dropped out of one society or another had done so before they reached their fifteenth birthday. These figures, however, must be treated with caution. In the first place they were affected by the total age structure (Appendix II, Tables 1 and 2) of the 939 boys and girls concerned; and secondly they included the leaving of those societies which set out to cater for young children. At the same time many of these societies had a senior section and the youngster could have gone into it had he wished.

Although the break occurred at about the age of leaving school (which for the majority was when they were just fifteen) the three groups of investigators were not agreed that the youngster left his society because he left school. The Oxfordshire enquirers certainly did find that the two matters were associated in the villages. They instanced the Grammar School children who retained their membership of an organization to a later age than did the rest of the adolescents. London however noted two possibly relevant points. In the first place the joining age for many of the well-known London clubs was fourteen; and secondly, 'leakage' from the organizations was always heavy in the first year of membership, irrespective of age. Some of the more vocal Nottingham youngsters were clear in their own mind that they had left their Guides, Sunday School and similar institutions simply because they had outgrown them. They seemed to feel quite strongly that they owed it to themselves to proceed to a more advanced state. This point is discussed later.

Among the two in three of the boys and girls who did not belong to any youth organization certain points stood out. The assertion that young wage earners often have domestic responsibilities which prevent them from joining an organization was not found to be true for the youngsters with whom the Enquiry was concerned. London hardly mentioned the subject and Oxfordshire merely observed that the journey to work, which so many of the village boys and girls had to make, seemed to be the only irrevocable thing that cut heavily into their leisure. A good many of the Nottingham girls were responsible for household chores on certain nights of the week and did not wriggle out of them; while some of the boys said they always undertook a certain job (chopping the firewood perhaps, or staying in to look after the baby) on the night that their father and mother went to the pictures or the pub. Such ties were not very onerous, however; and they were outweighed as far as free time was concerned by the very brief journey to work required of the majority of the boys and girls. Those who were really pressed for time included the Grammar School children and apprentices who had to spend two or even three nights a week at evening classes; but only one in eight of the Nottingham youngsters came into these two categories.

Another kind of youngster who, as Nottingham and Oxfordshire noticed, seldom attached himself to a youth organization, was the ardent sportsman and the real votary of any one hobby. The former tended to join a specialized society, like a boxing club or a works cricket club or an adult cycling club that admitted a certain number of adolescents. These sport lovers, practically all of them boys, were steady-going individuals with interests that did not fluctuate much. It was worth noting that, in Nottingham anyhow, they were almost the only adolescents who joined an organization by themselves. Presumably their game or hobby so carried them away that they lost the diffidence about facing a strange set of people which bedevilled so many of the youngsters. Another one-interest type of boy was the ardent fisherman, a solitary individual who, with his four-legged box and his bundle of rods, would go off by himself for a day on the Trent. These anglers had never mixed much with other children. They had a few, long-established pals, but little use for clubs and none at all for the interviewers. It was not that these sport-loving or one-hobby youngsters felt themselves superior to youth organizations: but they knew precisely what they wanted to do in their free time, and had enough enterprise to go out and get it for themselves.

Another batch of youngsters, however, certainly did regard youth organizations as beneath them in that they found them over-juvenile. One member of the London survey team went so far as to say he thought a good many of the boys gave allegiance to the societies only in so far as they were amused by them. Many of the more mature-minded boys and girls were impatient of any group in which a considerable proportion of the members were a good deal younger than themselves. They disparaged programmes which had to include provision for juvenile tastes. The old, old failing of youth work was observed more than once. The group, set up to cater for adolescents, was ineffective and the membership dropped. To pull up numbers the age limit was lowered. Younger children flooded in and, by their mere presence, drove out what remained of the adolescents. A case in point was that of a girl who had been an enthusiastic member of a uniformed unit from the time she was eleven to fourteen. Then the unit was invaded by children of eleven and twelve. The helpers, who were too few anyhow, turned to the fourteen-year-olds for help with this shoal of juniors. That was sound: but they neglected to provide more advanced work for the older members, and within a year the girl in question had left. The leader argued that had the girl been patient she could have gone up into the adult section of the organization when she was sixteen, disregarding the fact that at this age to stand still for a whole year is like a death sentence.

Nottingham also observed that the Grammar School adolescent joined special interest societies (such as a sailing club or a drama group) rather than a youth organization, partly because the former's level of work and its equipment were more adequate. The more able of the Secondary Modern School youngsters did not move in circles where societies of this kind existed, but at the same time they were bright enough to feel themselves a cut above the standards of many of the local youth groups. They did not exactly despise the latter's activities but they were impatient of inefficiencies and could not stomach the slow pace and restrictions inevitable in an organization that has to cater for all and sundry. In a way their outlook was similar to that of the Technical School girl of whom the staff complained that she was anti-social because she preferred a Saturday morning class in dress-designing to representing the school at hockey. These more able youngsters had enough wits and social acumen to make a reasonably sound use of their leisure according to their own inclinations. Some of them, of course, did join a youth group—but only as a stepping stone. They liked it very much for a time; but they out-grew it more quickly than the average member. A typical example was a boy called Barrie. He came from a rough and ready home but an intelligent one, in which the parents used to discuss ideas, as such, with the children. His own I.Q. was 113, and he had hobbies galore—rabbit-breeding, bird-watching and any money-making job he could put his hand to. He joined the Scouts when he was eleven, fell out with them, and left when he was twelve. He also fell out with a club that he joined in the following year. Then he attached himself to a uniformed organization and was a useful member, but only until he was fifteen. The boy could have been dismissed as one who never stuck to anything, a typical example of 'wastage'. What shook this theory was that both his school and his home record were exceedingly good. He was very responsible towards his four younger brothers and sisters, as well as to his parents who had serious domestic troubles. The difficulty about the youth groups he had joined was that he kept on outgrowing the group's level and had sufficient wits to realize this and to attach himself, stage by stage, to more advanced company.

Courting was another example of more mature tastes which clashed horribly with youth groups. Technical difficulties were often involved here. The organization to which the boy belonged might not be a mixed one; or the girl found that her new boy friend was too old for the group of which she was a member. Then there were well-worn customs. Courting couples were expected to be seen together at the pictures and the fair and the pantomime, and if they were not observing this traditional code (which did not include such a relative innovation as the youth organization) perhaps the courtship was not flourishing. In any case two's company and the finer shades of romance cannot be expected to flower amid the bottled effervescence of a youth group. In other words the girl, whether she was maturer than her contemporaries or merely more precocious, was confident that a youth organization does not really belong to the adult world of which serious courting is a hall mark.

If the more advanced youngster had little use for the youth groups the same was true of the adolescent who was noticeably below the general level of the area. It was these poorer boys and girls, poor in every sense, who so often said of the organizations 'I'm not interested'—a polite way of telling the interviewer that they had not the slightest intention of joining one. Oxford noted that these particular youngsters often came from homes where family conditions were likely to have caused emotional upset, or that they had suffered since childhood from some physical disability. London, too, spoke of the below-average boys and girls (perhaps amounting to twenty-five per cent of the Secondary Modern School population) who could not fit into any normal youth group. They were often of poor intelligence and in low grade jobs. Girls who were in unskilled routine factory work, for example, belonged to organizations less often than the clerical workers.* Among the non-joiners were those who were emotionally unstable, or who came from homes that, even to the casual observer, were most indifferently run. They had played on doorsteps and in gutters as toddlers (because they were a nuisance inside the overcrowded homes); they had roamed the streets for hours on end in childhood; and now they were in their teens they

*GIRLS' MEMBERSHIP OF ORGANIZATIONS
LONDON—Northbury and Camdington

	Total	Belong	Do not Belong
Typists, Clerks and Telephonists	38	19	19
Operatives and Factory hands	37	10	27
Machinists, Tailors, Dressmakers	27	5	22
Shop Assistants and Waitresses	5	1	4
Not Classified	9	—	9
	116	35	81

had not the discipline that is essential in order to be a member of any worth-while society. Nor had they had enough home training to pursue any interest or hobby regularly. In London's view some of them were the potential recruits or actual members of semi-criminal gangs. It also held for Nottingham, that many of the non-members were below par on a variety of counts, including those who had indifferent health. The pale wafer of a girl who had probably been as peaky-looking a child as was her small sister to-day, seldom belonged to an organization. Even the clothes of the below-average youngster were not up to local standards. On the whole the very scruffily dressed boy did not belong, nor did the schoolgirl who, even by fourteen, had not enough acumen to have grown beyond the be-socked, be-draggled and gum-chewing stage. On the other hand, there was no evidence that poor clothes as such stopped youngsters from joining. Then there were the mental dullards, those whom the school had put into its practical classes and whom the enquirers, from the first doorstep contact, had found uncommonly stupid. Emotionally unstable individuals are harder to identify than those with physical handicaps and the interviewers made no claims to accurate judgments. They did think, however, that a typical non-joiner of this class was the seventeen-year-old boy who was still so tied to his mother's apron strings that he hardly went out of the house by himself; and the girl who was invariably at loggerheads with her current job, forewoman and workmates. Another non-joiner was the one who, when his 'boys only' set had eventually dissolved, made no friends among girls but turned back to his home for all his emotional satisfactions. He was becoming progressively less and less able to face external company whether this involved a formal youth organization or merely a self-constituted group.

The below-average home, in so far as it affected the more obvious activities of the current generation of children, was relatively easy to spot. Certain of the families never bothered to send their children to such things as Sunday School or Brownies with any regularity. In these homes the child's spending money was a hit and miss affair. If the boy whined long enough he got his sixpence with or without the slap. Toddlers sat about on the step and played in the street all day; the older children's bed-time was any time; the mother could never say when the adolescent girl would be at home. Nothing seemed to be planned in advance by these families. Their homes had a general air of insecurity with the uncertain meals and the cheerlessness that accompanies this. The adolescents from these families had two characteristics that were particularly relevant to the Enquiry. Teachers remembered them as children with little staying power, while the leaders of any organization they had belonged to recalled that they had never had the persistence to pursue an activity to its end. Secondly they were noticeably bad mixers and indeed their inability to make new friends was publicly recognized. Nor was this just a phase of adolescence for, as children, they had never had a particular set of street friends nor, later on, had they ever wriggled their way into a school clique. They did lay claim to *some* friends, of course, but they made them according to a more rigid pattern than did the other boys and girls. Either they had no friends outside their family, or they tied themselves exclusively to one other youngster, or they only went about with a tight little set, most of whom had been buddies since they had first played in the street. The social ill-ease of these particular boys and girls was reflected in their relations with the interviewers. They were tongue-tied to a degree, while the adults of their homes as a rule adopted an unhelpful attitude. It was not only the youth organizations which made so little impact on the below-average families. Social workers and health visitors also despaired of them. The officials of the Churches might or might not know the household by name, but they seldom had any contact with the adolescent members even when they had known them as Sunday School children. The large size of many of these families and the indifferent training that they gave their children, likewise made them a trial to most of their neighbours. The fact that they lived by a rather different set of standards from those of most of the neighbourhood isolated them from its daily life. They tended to congregate in certain streets or parts of

CONCLUSIONS

a street, and indeed the 'bad' families almost seemed to pick each other out. In their small and highly local world, tradition doubtless played an important part. Any hostility towards persons or societies was probably transmitted down succeeding generations of adolescents, and it is not unlikely that they and their parents equated the youth organization with authority in the shape of the School, the Church and the Law. This would be especially likely in the case of the latter, since youngsters on probation are so often required to attend a youth group.

On the whole the girls made less use of societies than did their brothers (Appendix II, Table 2). In the Oxfordshire villages the girls, after they had reached fourteen, dropped out of the society rather more often than did the boys. In Robin Wood effective membership was less common among the girls of adolescent age than among the boys; and only seven out of the sixty-five girls were active members for the whole eighteen months of the Enquiry. The older Robin Wood girls, those aged sixteen and over, belonged less often than those in their early teens. This did not hold for Northbury, however, where the proportion was about equal; nor for Camdington where the older girls belonged rather more frequently than those of fourteen and fifteen. The one aspect of membership that was common to both town and country was that the girls who were preoccupied with courting and its preliminaries had little time, in any sense of the word, for youth organizations. Some of the younger girls probably joined a mixed organization because they hoped to meet an assortment of boys there; but their membership was liable to be a precarious one. In Robin Wood any girl who was courting hard could almost be guaranteed not to belong to a youth organization.

Why did the girls react so differently from the boys? In the first place, facilities for sport and physical activities were a major interest of most of the boys; and the youth organizations provided such essentials as equipment, pitches and teams. Only a minority of the girls had played enough outdoor games at school to become sufficiently proficient to continue with them without a good deal of encouragement. The absorbing interest for them was to experiment with their personal appearance, and this they could best do at home, aided perhaps by one or two onlookers. The girls' friendship habits, too, were rather different from those of the boys. When they started work their school gangs dissolved more quickly than those of the boys. For the first few months therefore they often lacked companions with whom to break into any new and possibly hostile group. Even if they did retain one dear friend, the pair of them had to be of a mind about trying out any organization. The more dependent partner was always liable to be nervous about making new acquaintances, since these might well threaten her own future. The village girls but not, apparently, those in towns, were more discriminating than the boys about the company they kept. They summed up a group's social level more finely than their brothers, and attached more importance to it. As young women they appreciated the effort required to maintain high physical standards in a house or a personal appearance; and they were not prepared to sink to the level of a group which paid scant attention to such things. The Oxfordshire enquirers also found girls who were non-joiners coming from a home which was likely to have caused emotional disturbance, i.e. where the parents had separated or where the mother was a shockingly bad housekeeper.

These adolescent girls of working class homes were in general required to perform two duties. In the first place their parents expected them to hold the fort in any domestic crisis that might threaten the earning power of the males and the older women of the family. It was the young girl worker (and not her brother, mother or school-girl sister) who was kept at home if anyone in the house was ill. Secondly she was expected to make a satisfactory marriage and to be reasonably quick about it. In Robin Wood, for example, from 'having a boy' to 'going steady', and from 'going steady' to 'getting married', were the proper steps for any dutiful daughter to take in her teens and to have completed by her early twenties. A girl who was sufficiently attractive and proper-spirited to proceed by this pattern, brought credit to all. Aunties and uncles and grandparents were involved since relatives were often as ambitious as parents that the girl should make a good match. Social ambition of this type was not uncommon, and meant that the family might openly encourage a girl who was still in her middle teens to keep clear of any company that might threaten her chances of meeting a nice boy with a good job. The girl herself was probably less bothered about these aspirations than with more personal concerns, the calls of romance and pride, the delectable possibilities of a home of her own and of the day that would transform her from just 'Johnson's girl' into 'the lady on the top floor'. The picture may have been overdrawn but it held good for a considerable number of the steady-going girls (as well as the more highly-sexed young women) who happened to have ambitious relatives.

At least two points distinguished these still-under-eighteen artisan-bred girls from those of families with a professional background. The first was that, whatever the girl's personal tastes, her family expected her to be on the look-out for marriage. Secondly they envisaged her marrying relatively soon, aware, no doubt, that to-day's girls are marrying at an earlier age than their mothers did.* A daughter brought up on such lines was highly likely to consider that a youth organization was irrelevant to anyone who was almost grown-up. The more lively and boy-conscious young women went off to the public dance halls, ice rinks, speedway tracks and occasionally to pubs—places where they would meet men rather older than themselves. The equally boy-conscious but less up-and-coming girls who were nervous about facing any new group transferred their affections soon after they left school from their one girl friend to one boy; or sometimes they managed to keep both in tow. The point with all these girls was that a youth organization represented so different a *kind* of relationship from any which they recognized as proper for one nearly adult, that the

---

* *The* 1951 *Census one per cent sample* shows that the proportion of women in England and Wales who marry at the ages of 15–19 has increased since 1931 from 1·3 to 4·5 per cent; at the ages of 20–24 from 5·8 to 48·4 per cent. 61,000 married before the age of 20. Of all women aged 20–24 about an equal number are married as single.

idea of joining did not seriously enter their heads.

That was how the girls saw it. As for the organizations, the well-rooted boys' club seldom had a parallel society that had anything like such influence among the local girls. The effective organizations available for young women were the uniformed ones and the members of these were mainly school children. Indeed in all three areas the really popular society for girls of adolescent age was uncommon. Even when the unit was a mixed one, it was more often related to the tastes and needs of boy members than of girls. The Upper Hinton Club was a case in point. Although originally set up to provide for all the adolescents of the village it was primarily a boys' society. The girls were aware of this. They pointed out that socials, dances and expeditions, the affairs in which girls as well as boys took part, were not regular events and that even the drama group did not meet all the year round. The girls could certainly borrow library books and play table tennis; but the stock activities were the boys' indoor games like billiards and darts and, more important, the boys' football and cricket. The London enquirers observed another aspect of this emphasis on masculine needs, viz. that when a mixed unit had to cut down its programme it was the girls' activities which were jettisoned. The girls were alleged to be more difficult to understand that the boys, less ready to take part in group activities and altogether less clubable. Moreover, to move to more urgent matters, the police had much less trouble with the girls; so that even the claim that youth organizations stave off delinquency weakened the cause of the weaker sex. Although the more perspicacious youth worker is perhaps a trifle sceptical of the notion that girls are really more moral than their brothers, official publicity about youth work always emphasizes its value to the boy; and those parents who favour youth organizations on principle for their sons, often regard them as pointless institutions as far as girls are concerned. Indeed one or two of the more old-fashioned Robin Wood mothers considered it unsuitable for their adolescent daughters to join a society of any kind, and one with lads in it was definitely suspect.

CONCLUSIONS 117

CONCLUSIONS RELATING TO THE YOUTH ORGANIZATIONS

The enquirers analysed certain features of the units they met which appeared to deter the local youngster from joining them. These features did not hold good for all the units, but they were sufficiently widespread to affect the total membership figures. Some of these issues lay within the control of the unit itself, others did not. Among the former was the age structure of the groups which were definitely setting out to cater for those at the adolescent stage. In all three areas, comment from the boys and girls themselves suggested that certain of them regarded the local organizations as too juvenile for their taste. This came out so strongly in the Nottingham Pilot Enquiry that the age structure of the units which the Robin Wood youngsters were likely to join was examined in some detail. The figures were as follows. As has been said earlier, thirty-six groups open to boys and girls aged fourteen to seventeen were situated within a quarter of an hour's walk of all the youngsters. Approximately 700 boys and 480 girls aged under fifteen, and 600 boys and 300 girls aged fifteen and over, belonged to these units; so that as far as total *membership* went the organizations were weighted on the side of the younger ones. A snap sample (Appendix II, Table 4) of one week's *attendance* figures at ten of the units revealed a similar emphasis, viz. that more youngsters aged fourteen (and in this case fifteen too) were actually present, in that particular week, than those aged sixteen and seventeen. It is rash to draw too rigid a deduction from figures of this kind, because the unit's own structure (e.g. its provision for those under and over adolescent age) may affect the membership of those aged fourteen to seventeen. But quite apart from figures, the picture that the organizations presented on their ordinary nights and at their displays, was one of schoolgirls and schoolboys rather than of young workers of sixteen and seventeen. The emphasis was not all that evident—not to the casual visitor—but it certainly would have been to the age-analysing eye of any sixteen-year-old, casting round for a possible set with whom to associate. It has been pointed out that those youngsters who had rather more mature tastes than their friends made little use of the organizations: and that the below-average individuals, and those girls who were much occupied with courting, kept out on a variety of grounds. This left the middle kind; but they, as the observations on 'Friends' have stressed, made their particular cronies among people of about their own age. It is difficult to judge whether discrepancy in age was a genuine deterrent to the older boys' and girls' membership; but, in view of that zeal for the age just beyond one's own (which is a hall-mark of adolescence), it appeared to be a point which the organizations should have examined if they wished to cater primarily for adolescents.

In London the conditions that certain of the Church units attached to membership was another feature that stopped some of the youngsters from joining. These charges against the Church units were practically confined to London. They showed far less in Robin Wood although two-thirds of the units were connected with Churches. Nor did they appear in the villages where Church membership and weekday activities were commonly interwoven. Many of the London boys and girls averred that they had left such units because it meant compulsory attendance at Church; or because they had to go to Sunday School; or to be confirmed; or to belong to the Choir. Local adults sometimes bore out what the youngsters said. For example, an official of a Borough Council said that boys and girls often told her that they had stopped going to one society or another 'because of religion'. Even when the youngsters did not mention a specific membership condition, they often believed, rightly or wrongly, that the recreational group was just a bait to lure them into the Church. This exacerbated them. They contended that they were not going to have religion rammed down their throats like that. Of course the hostility may well have been less due to membership conditions than to the unit's ineffectiveness as an organization. One member at least of the London Team thought that some of the clergy did not take youth groups seriously; and another member observed that totally unsuitable adults were sometimes entrusted with the running of a group because this was a form of service. Or the trouble may have been connected with the fact that so many of the Church groups were old-established ones, dating from the time when it was only the Churches that bothered about the recreation of young workers. Apprehensive, and a little jealous of the newer secular groups, they deliberately emphasized their traditional conditions of membership, forgetting that children's upbringing has undergone radical changes; that it is less authoritarian than it was; and above all that the majority of the grown-ups whom to-day's adolescents respect and love have no connection with a Church. The sort of youngster who had made such charges as the above had obviously not found the precise kind of fun and games that he had expected in the organization and had not waited to see if the more sober side of the programme had anything to offer. So large a number of adolescents took this line that the following observations on the general attitude of the boys and girls to formal religion may not be out of place.

Their relationship with their local Churches appeared to be roughly as follows. The great majority had been in contact with a Church in the past, chiefly through Sunday School. Many of the Londoners recalled the village Sunday Schools they had gone to regularly when they were evacuated; but said they had not continued with Sunday School when they came back to Northbury or Camdington. In Nottingham the adolescents' younger brothers and sisters mostly attended Church, or Sunday School. The same was true for the younger Oxfordshire children, as well as for those adolescents who were still at school and indeed for many who had left. In both the urban areas however the majority of the adolescents had no longer any effective link with a Church. In Northbury very few of those interviewed had been to any Church or Sunday School on the previous Sunday; while in Robin Wood only eleven youngsters of a hundred and seventeen who told how they had spent the last seven days mentioned a Church or Sunday School attendance. General observation of the Nottingham youngsters over a period of two years confirmed what this sample figure suggested. As soon as the boys and girls started to work they began to change over to the Robin Wood adult pattern, i.e. they knew the Churches and Chapels by sight, their chief officials by name, but had no personal truck with either. Most of those adolescents who did go to religious services were connected with a Free Church in the heart of the area. This Church had no resident minister but depended on a very hard-working set of young adults who ran the Sunday School and a series of vigorous week-night societies—Scouts, Guides, a Youth Fellowship with a Tennis Club—in addition to week-end and holiday camps.

Quite apart from such a thing as Church attendance, many of the Robin Wood adolescents seemed unfamiliar with traditional Christian lore. No one, in a group of eight of the girls, appeared to recognize the name of Wesley, nor did 'Lead Kindly Light' strike a chord. In a Church they visited, the altar was described as the place where 'you come up here and they make you eat like a white pill'—and so on. It was also possible for a set as old as sixteen and seventeen to have a lengthy argument as to whether Roman Catholics were Christians, and eventually to decide that they were not.

The Northbury interviewers were so struck by the youngsters' attitude to the Churches, and to religion generally, that they paid special attention to this subject among the families of the Camdington boys and girls. They found that, while few of the parents were anti-religious, the great majority had no positive interest in religion. The same appeared to hold true of Robin Wood though there it was noticeable how many parents definitely liked their children to go to Sunday School. This was more than a matter of getting rid of the family. Sunday School was regarded as a good thing for the child; and many mothers went to a good deal of trouble to get dinner over and the children spruced up and to see that they attended regularly. It was also noticeable how often the less satisfactory adolescents came from homes where the current generation of younger children were not steady Sunday School goers. In other words Sunday School attendance still seemed to be a good yard-stick.

The Camdington boys and girls frequently dismissed religion

as a subject in which they were not interested; but the enquirers recognized that this might be no more than a superficial reaction, the easy reply to two or three questions from a stranger. All the same, when the relationship between the adult and the adolescent was on a deeper level, it seemed safe to assume that some adolescents practically never thought about spiritual or moral questions in any guise. Some of the Robin Wood youngsters, for example, said in a surprised sort of way that such topics never entered their minds; and if pursued they found them excitingly novel. Their nearest approach to a non-material world seemed to be books about witchcraft and the supernatural happenings of which they read in their magazines and Sunday papers. One thing that the Nottingham interviewers noticed was how seldom the youngsters referred spontaneously to the school's teaching and practice of religion. They did not appear to connect their daily service or their Religious Instruction lessons with Church membership, nor indeed with the subject of religion. On the other hand, certain of the boys and girls were beginning to be aware of the deeper issues of life. Several of the steady Church-goers had to put up with a good deal of chaff from their contemporaries. Of the older boys, one couple who had thought a lot about religion had decided to 'become atheists'.

As far as a mere surface-level investigation could ascertain, this indifference to the Church and to religion was patently a reflection of the adult world in which these boys and girls moved. In this world modernity carried enormous weight; and one of the youngsters' most frequent criticisms was that the Churches were not up-to-date. Only very old people 'like my Grandma' could be expected to take an interest in such old-fashioned and therefore melancholy affairs. Some of the Churches referred to have depressing exteriors; and except for a few hours on Sunday they certainly are the most dead-alive looking buildings in the area. One of the Northbury complaints was that the clergy thought of themselves as belonging to a higher social class, and did not know how to come down to the level of ordinary men. The hint of condescension was resented. This accusation was possibly related to a point observed in Robin Wood, that those who belonged to the Church organizations were slightly above the social level of the area. Certainly the really low-level families were mostly quite untouched by the Church youth groups. As has been said before, most of the Robin Wood adolescents had no personal relationship with the local parsons and ministers; nor did the latter seem to know many of the Enquiry families even by name. This situation is not confined to Nottingham, of course; and is perhaps partly due to the fact that whereas in the past it was the local Church which tried to cope with the troubles of the poorer homes, to-day a professional, non-resident and above all a transitory population of civil servants undertakes many of these jobs.

In general the situation seemed to be something like this. The adult world of these boys and girls made no pretence to formal religious observance. Nor had their artisan world as yet begun to reflect any intelligent concern with formal religion. At the same time new moral codes, and new techniques in the upbringing of children (popularized by the press and the radio as well as practised in the schools) made these working class parents strongly opposed to the idea of subjecting their children to force about anything, church-going included. What sounds like reasoned argument may, of course, have been no more than an excuse to avoid the bother of training a child, but it was noticed how often the parent would say 'We were *made* to go, and we're not going to do the same to him'. Those adolescents who belonged to a Church mostly did so from their own conviction. In a sense they were pioneers. While the conversion of the sixteen-year-old Nottingham bred William Booth appeared to have no parallels among to-day's adolescents, the youngsters had enough sense of the implications of religion to be genuinely averse to making it a mere formality—as it seemed to them it was when Church-going was demanded by a youth organization as so much payment for a game of football. Some of those who seemed so blind to spiritual issues were obviously handicapped by their extreme ignorance, not only of the externals but of the essential framework of Christian theology. Indeed there appeared to be a case for a popular strictly factual book about Christianity.

As regards the vexed question of attaching strings to membership, the interviewers bore in mind that the Church is the oldest partner in youth work. On numerical grounds alone it is still probably the strongest, although, as was found in Oxfordshire, certain areas appear to have no special policy about their work with adolescents. But the Church youth groups had more significant assets than numbers and years. Their leaders were very conscious that the adolescents' organization was part of a larger society, and this gave them a conscious aim. Despite all these advantages, however, the Church units on the whole appeared to make no more effective an attack than the secular ones on the below-average adolescents, on the bad streets, on the bottom level homes and on the delinquent-breeding areas. Nor did they realize the sheer ineffectiveness of attaching strings that were out of keeping with current thought. Moreover, to recognize the principle of the 'open' unit (as some said they did) by inviting in everyone, provided everyone was of the unit's way of thinking, was the kind of dishonesty that the youngsters scented at once. Since religion is more often caught than taught, the really effective string was the youngsters' and their families' sound personal relationship with adults who did belong to a Church. It seemed to the enquirers that in a world where material values are so terrifyingly dominant, the importance of this relationship could not be over-emphasized.

The final conclusion reached on this subject was that to-day spiritual issues might be more readily brought to the notice of adolescents in general through secular rather than religious societies. Although neither type touches a considerable proportion of youngsters, many of those who have no personal contact with the officers of their local Churches do at least get on friendly terms with their youth leaders. Should this policy be sound the magnitude of the youth organization's task, in the face of so much ignorance and apathy, should be recognized. The presentation of religion to boys and girls who have not experienced it in their homes requires not only a knowledge of the subject and an understanding of adolescents but also outstanding gifts of leadership. Where these gifts are displayed in a unit which is well organized from the more material point of view, they undoubtedly meet a genuine need. There was plenty of evidence from the organizations themselves that many young people found a deep and unexpected satisfaction in a religious way of life.

One perspicacious observer noted that it was seldom the *fashion* among the youngsters to belong to a youth organization. The London interviewers found that the organizations themselves were not always abreast of the times. Too many of the buildings were battered and paintless outside, cold and comfortless within. One club visited was described as follows. 'The five rooms were large, dingy, cheerless and perishingly cold . . . The canteen . . . was the only moderately warm room in the place, also it was the only one with chairs. Elsewhere people were sitting on the floor. Two of the youngsters were shiveringly trying to play chess over a minute gas fire in the office.' In Oxfordshire the premises and equipment were frequently second-rate; and though Nottingham did not echo this complaint, all three areas stressed the disparity between the physical appearance of the places where the youngsters were invited to spend their free time and the rising standards of their schools, work rooms and homes. The youth unit's difficulties over premises are too well known for this Report to labour the point. The enquirers themselves saw how often the organizations had to make do with ramshackle and antiquated rooms because these were the cheap ones or, in the bombed areas, the only ones available. The units were perpetually short of money for repairs and replacements although they tended to have dreadfully destructive occupants. None of which, however, really excused the untidiness and the general messiness of certain of the premises. Indeed some of the boys' groups seemed to glory in this and to regard it as an outward and visible sign of internal manliness. To judge by their scathing comments the youngsters were often more intelligent on this point than their betters. They knew how much hard work and sheer force of character is required to create a pleasant environment with only a thin purse. And they

CONCLUSIONS

probably sensed that just as the externals of a civilized life—warmth, light, cleanliness, order—encourage decent behaviour so dark entries, bombed sites, squalid cafés and dirt and disorder in any guise induce the jungle level. In other words the youth group that disregarded the example which its own appearance set was, to say the least of it, educationally behind the times. The same held for games and tools of which a good many of the units were extremely short. It was difficult to see what good the leaders hoped to achieve merely by getting a crowd of adolescents into a building. Not to provide them with a reasonable supply of equipment seemed a complete waste of effort. It meant that the youngsters had not enough to do, they grew bored, they got rowdy and the jungle level was there again. Some of the boys met had far better equipment for their games and hobbies at home than those at their youth groups; and they only came to the latter to idle away a night. The root of the problem of course is lack of money and man-power. Many units have an annual budget, to cover all needs, which would be insufficient to redecorate one small suburban house.

The same criticism, that certain of the organizations were not abreast of the times, held for their programmes. Oxfordshire found that some of the units seemed to be quite unfamiliar with the standard of work done in the schools, and so made no attempt to build up from what the youngsters had already learnt. The units' activities were not exacting enough to stimulate real effort, and their goals were over simple. This criticism was less common in sport and in physical culture than in an occupation like handicrafts. Here the London enquirers thought that the units did not take advantage of a vague but widespread demand among the boys and girls to 'make things'. Too much reliance was placed on the teaching of crafts in weekly classes. Ready as the London County Council and other Education Authorities were to provide instructors, a class was not necessarily the best way in which to catch and deepen what was often no more than a tentative interest. The Nottingham enquirers were impressed by the skilful and imaginative crafts that so many of the schools taught. It also observed that even the below-average boys and girls who had left school often did bits of craft work at home. Girls, for example, embroidered, though less adventurously than at school; they knitted, and they drew stylish ladies in billowing dresses. The boys repaired fishing rods, they made and sold model planes, they built up their cycles. But most of them lacked ideas, many were short of tools and nearly all were hard put for space. As one mother phrased it, there comes a time when no home can accommodate a shipwright. The real enthusiasts took themselves off to classes; but those who were less skilled manually, and above all those who were socially backward, would not face the competition and the new personal relationships which classes and clubs involved. Another deterrent was that the more boy-conscious of the girls would seldom pin themselves down to a weekly class for fear that the following week it might clash with more important things. If next Tuesday a boy should whistle, they must be free to come to him. To overcome difficulties of this kind the Nottingham enquirers proposed as an experiment that a youngsters' own workshop should be set up. Such an institution might possibly encourage more handwork and this would be of therapeutic value to the below-average adolescent[*] as well as help to meet the perennial demand for tools and working space from the one who was relatively skilled but handicapped by a congested, gardenless and shedless home. This subject is referred to more fully on p. 147.

Although the interviewers found that the provision for sport was less inadequate than that for hobbies, they did feel that the units failed to meet the constant plea from boys for more facilities for self-run games. The London and Nottingham interviewers both came across boys who, in the face of many difficulties, organized their own football teams. They encountered a host of smaller groups who could have entertained themselves with scratch games of football and cricket all the year round if they had had anywhere to play. To encourage these little informal sets might be criticized as pandering to the boy who had not enough

[*] *Unravelling Juvenile Delinquency.* Glueck. The Commonwealth Fund, New York, 1950.

moral stamina to try to get into a club team. But these scratch games gave a lot of pleasure and exercise to the physical weaklings who never could have got themselves into any team. Certainly it was *play* rather than a *game*, but who would gainsay its value on that account? In Northbury and Camdington, girls' athletics were very poorly catered for. Hardly any of the units took advantage of the fact that nowadays all senior schools play outdoor games. It was not merely that many of the girls missed the pleasure of their netball and rounders, their gym and their dancing, but that any physical activities would have been so excellent for them since they were frequently in jobs where they got much less fresh air and exercise than they had been accustomed to. The units, however, appeared to work on the old theory that girls were too tired after work to take part in anything strenuous. The plea, of course, is largely irrelevant to-day, what with better feeding and more healthy working conditions. The free Saturday and Sunday, that two-sevenths of the week which gives the opportunity for positive recreation as distinct from desultory rest, was likewise disregarded by a good many of the organizations. Certain of the boys met did not reckon to get up on Saturday and Sunday till middle day. What was there to get up for, they said. Nor did the youth groups as a rule take advantage of bicycles, the one piece of equipment that nearly everyone possessed or could borrow. Few of the units encouraged long-distance cycling at the week-end, as distinct from just pottering around the local streets. In the glorious June weather when the Northbury Enquiry was undertaken, hardly any of these able-bodied boys and girls who were living in such unfavourable conditions went off to camps or Youth Hostels. Some of the Church units would not encourage such expeditions because it took the youngsters away from their own place of worship; but considering the tiny proportion of adolescents who ever attended a religious service the excuse was irrelevant for the organizations as a whole.

Another small example of failure to keep abreast of the times was the units' disregard of the fact that a larger proportion of children now attend Grammar Schools. Harnessed to their homework, these school children may well require as careful consideration, when the unit's time-table is drawn up, as does the worker who is free every night on the stroke of five-thirty. Another failure was that some of them did not keep up with current educational practice as regards instilling in adolescents the rudiments of self-government. And how many of these adolescent groups seized on the fact that their members, as distinct from school children, were handling part of a weekly pay packet and one that was constantly getting fatter? The Oxfordshire enquirers observed wryly that a young wage earner's financial responsibilities to his own organization need not, in 1951, be confined to collecting salvage and running a jumble sale.

In all this the real point was that too often the organizations were not sensing current tastes. They failed signally to recognize the great weight that 'modernity' carries in the average artisan home, symbolizing as it does those things that the working class family of the past was only able to achieve by great self-scarifice, or by a fluke. 'Modern' was so vital a word to these boys and girls, and to most of the adults of their world, that it behoved any unit which professed to teach the good life to appear up-to-date itself. In so far as the youth organization's activities did not sound fashionable ones, in so far as its set-up was authoritarian and by implication old-fashioned, and in so far as its physical setting was slovenly, the unit lost respect. Moreover the first person to disparage any group that was not abreast of the times was the youngster from the home which was 'particular'—just the home, of course, that was an influential one among its neighbours.

The enquirers came to the conclusion that one of the most important points which affected the youngsters' joining of societies was the parents' relationship with the local youth organizations. Did parents know the units at first hand; and had they any idea of the more serious aims of these societies? As far as Northbury and Camdington were concerned, the answer was that although a good many of the local adults were somewhat worried about the habits of the rising generation, few of these grown-up people turned to the youth groups as a possible remedy; and they certainly felt under no obligation to assist any of the units themselves. The same held good for Oxfordshire and Nottingham. As was said earlier, none of the parents of the Robin Wood families played a regular part in any of the thirty-six local youth groups; and apparently not more than a handful of the two thousand adults of the area had any connection with a youth organization in other parts of the city. Yet practically all the Robin Wood groups were short of help: one or two had shut down for lack of leaders, several had a waiting list for juniors, and most had useful activities in mind which they were too short-staffed to introduce. The leaders were so overdriven in some cases that they had no time for any recreation at adult level for themselves. Those were matters of fact. Somewhat more conjectural were the parents' views on the local groups. There was a certain amount of mis-information, for example among old-fashioned mothers who feared that a mixed society was not safe for girls, and among brawny fathers who alleged that a uniformed society took the guts out of a boy of spirit. These, however, were in the minority. But very few parents had any conception that a youth group might relieve them of their troubles over their offspring, such as the father who worried because his girl stayed out so late on the Hill, or the widow who would have liked her sixteen-year-old son to have a man's control. The Nottingham interviewers, and to some extent those in London, made the point that while the purpose of school was accepted as beneficial by parents, that of the youth organization (except in its negative aspect) was quite unrecognized. The shoe also pinched on the other foot, for some of the leaders were not over-familiar with the parents' ambitions for their children and especially as to what things the less vocal families set store by. The enquirers felt that it was as important for the leader to know something of these goals as to be conversant with the family background; though, this too, was often unknown on the curious assumption that a family tree, unless bad, somehow loses its significance as the social scale falls.

 Would the local adults have been of much use to the organizations? In the eyes of the Nottingham enquirers the answer was definitely 'yes'. Many of the parents were capable and reliable people who were not unduly pressed for time, and who had a genuine desire for their youngsters to learn just the things for which the youth organization stood; as, for example, the father who strongly approved of his son belonging to the St. John Ambulance Brigade because this was teaching the boy to do things for other people without expecting to be paid. Certain of the parents had skills and hobbies of their own which they were quite intelligent enough to pass on to two or three youngsters although they could not have faced a class. It was difficult to find a single unit at which most of the adults would not have been of some help. Cooking and washing, equipment making, furniture mending, register keeping and notice writing—these are typical of the hundred and one small jobs which are terribly time-consuming for the leader, but which any sensible adult can prod the youngsters into doing for themselves—which is precisely what the leader wants.

It seemed desirable on other grounds that the local adults should play a larger part in the units. Apart from the genuine need for their services, they would have helped to establish the case for the youth organization to the youngster, whereas an occasional appeal from an external source was largely ineffective. What the more reluctant youngster needed was slight pressure from many people all the time. The more the adults of his own street were acquainted with the persons and in sympathy with the purposes of the local youth groups, the more local pressure would have suggested to him that it was the proper thing to belong to an organization.

There was another reason why home and youth group should work together. If the unit's aim was less to reflect the leader's own standards than the best of those that the neighbourhood revered, then the leader needed constant advice and check from the neighbourhood itself. To disregard local values was to copy one of the weaknesses of the Secondary Modern School which, if its staff all live away from the locality, *may* represent a set of values so foreign to certain of the children that they are almost meaningless. Youth organizations, even more than schools, have always had to face the difficulty that the youngsters' parents and neighbours may regard the organization as an external institution. In former days it probably represented benevolence provided by the rich for the poor; and to-day it may well represent a service provided by an Education Authority or a Church or a firm. Whoever the provider, it is seldom those people whose homes stand alongside the society's meeting place and whose children are asked to conform to its teachings. Many of the units which the enquirers met had overcome such difficulties manfully, and were accepted as an integral part of the local community; but others had no more than an alien standing and were disregarded primarily on this ground.

Practical issues were involved in drawing in the local adults. There was the question of time. Many people were far too busy; but some of those with grown-up families and some of the childless couples had a good deal of leisure. In particular, the elder brothers and sisters of the adolescent* often led a relatively leisured life compared to the voluntary leaders, most of whom ran their unit after a full day's work. Few of these potential helpers, however, had more than a limited number of hours to give; and the unit, like industry, had to adapt itself to very part-time labour. It was also sound policy to keep the initial plea for help on a small scale, and to clothe it in personal terms—a request by Mr. Jones who takes the Club's woodwork class, to Mr. Smith, whose nephew, it will be remembered, belongs to the Club's football team. The request had to be strictly utilitarian too, and perhaps no more exacting than whether Mr. Smith would come and show a couple of boys how to fix up some shelves.

As far as Robin Wood was concerned the enlistment of the local adult meant something like this. There was a fund of ability and goodwill, and a certain amount of leisure, among the relations and adult neighbours of the boys and girls. In general this goodwill was confined to their own domestic circle, except in the case of a few families connected with a Church or a political party. No plea of service to the Community, or to the Needs of the Younger Citizen, would have tapped it. A much more concrete approach

* *Voluntary Action.* Beveridge. Allen and Unwin, 1948.

was required; a personal request for a small service to a few youngsters over a limited period of time. To a busy leader the game might sound hardly worth the candle; but the point is that an artisan area like Robin Wood still relies on first hand contact for any significant communication, and no appreciable amount of help would have been forthcoming until this face to face approach had been made.

The boys' and girls' joining of societies appeared to be even more of a trial and error process than is the case with adults. Some of this was inevitable, and indeed desirable, but too many short term memberships were a nuisance to all concerned. 'Wastage', it is important to remember, may be as disheartening a business to the youngster as to the leader. Sometimes it was the recruiting methods of the organization which were at fault. A boy's typical retort to the question of why he did not belong to any group was that he had never been asked and hadn't bothered. Although this may have been no more than the easy answer, it quite often sounded like the truth—in which case it was a sobering reflection on the recruiting methods of the local units. The organization's normal technique seemed to be to cast its net and see what swam in. If reasonably efficient it got its numbers; but—and this was the important point—it drew them from the potential joiners of a fairly wide area, rather than the all and sundry of its immediate neighbourhood. Few of the units appeared to make any continuous effort to break down the resistance of the non-joiner whose home was on their own doorstep. Indeed, they seemed unaware of the number of adolescents who were living within five minutes' walk of their own building. Admittedly, too much parochialism is undesirable; but the point is that if youth groups are a sound institution for the normal youngster, then some of them somewhere should continually be trying to attract the two in three adolescents who, by the enquirers' finding, are still non-joiners. In any case why leave the initiative to the youngster? The London enquirers made much of the point that it was nobody's business to see that the youngster who would have patently benefited from a society was helped to find his way into one. It

CONCLUSIONS

found the uniformed organizations particularly at fault. In Northbury and Camdington they mostly expected the adolescent to seek them out;·and this in a locality where uniforms were suspect among the older boys, and regarded as childish and glamour-dispelling by all but a few of the girls. In view of what so many of those who did belong to uniformed organizations enjoyed about their units, London considered that the adolescent membership ought to have been higher. The Northbury St. John Ambulance Brigade was an instance of this. It had a small but loyal band of local supporters; it provided the opportunity for personal service that the more good-hearted youngster appreciated; and it had the goodwill of the public. But relatively few of the adolescents belonged to it or, for that matter, to the Northbury Scouts or Brigades or pre-Service organizations.

Then there was the question of recruiting in sets, rather than through the individual or through just the boy and his pal. It has already been pointed out how much importance the youngsters attached to their particular friends, especially in the case of those who relied on their own set as compensation for a below-average or affectionless home. The London enquirers observed that every block of flats had sets of boys who spent all their free time together. 'Buildings' and yards and cul-de-sac streets created similar loyalties, yet the recruiting schemes of youth leaders on the whole ignored them.

Another weakness of the organizations was that described as the induction crisis—how to help the newcomer feel that he mattered to at least one other person in the new group. The recruit was observed to encounter at least three types of fence. He might be so unlucky as to find himself in a group where the existing members tried on principle to freeze out strangers. Or he might get himself into company whose habits were familiar enough but where the adults, however perspicacious about fringe members, were too busy to give the inconspicuous coddling that the slow-witted youngster needs before he can adapt himself to new company. Over-rigid programmes, too, may run counter to the necessity to help the new member feel that he is more important than the table-tennis match. All the evidence suggested that joining is essentially a matter of a relationship between *persons*; but, as any leader knows, this is an exceedingly time-consuming business. Too often the leader cannot be more than a busy benevolent policeman. His organization must tick over, discipline must be assured, committees must be attended. All of which means that he does not get enough first-hand contact even with his regular members, and he certainly has not the time to try to build up a personal relationship with each newcomer.

The London investigators came to the conclusion that one of the answers to the above difficulties revolved round the question of someone fitting the right boy into the right group. The Nottingham enquirers made much of the same point, especially in view of the fact that it appeared to be social diffidence which stopped so many of the below-average Robin Wood boys and girls from venturing into any new world. It was plain that even the normal youngster was often at sea as to which was a suitable group for him. In the case of the less mature boy, if he did take the plunge he could not adjust himself as quickly as the average youngster, he felt left out, and sooner or later he left. In view of all this the Nottingham enquirers suggested that the youth organizations of a neighbourhood might appoint an honorary 'adviser' to act as liaison officer between them and the total adolescent population of a defined, not too large, area. This adviser would be knowledgeable about each of the local organizations but not be connected with any one of them. He would, therefore, be genuinely neutral as to which organization to suggest, whereas it is difficult for a leader to be entirely impartial since he must to some extent stand or fall by the numbers on his register and the effectiveness of his programme. Such an adviser would require to be sufficiently perspicacious to realize when a youngster was best left to follow his own devices. To help him he would have close links with the local schools, the Children's Department, the Probation Service, etc. A new type of youth worker on these lines may sound like an over-finicky luxury; but the Nottingham enquirers saw no other way of reaching the more difficult young-

CONCLUSIONS 135

ster than for the latter to have a regular contact with one person whose business it was to keep a friendly eye on him especially in regard to his joining of societies.

Oxfordshire treated this subject on broader lines than did London or Nottingham, but the interviewers there likewise felt the need for some person to act as a consultant to the adolescents. A good many of the boys and girls whom the interviewers met would have benefited from some kindly supervision for two or three years after leaving school. Some of this was related to their job, but they also needed the kind of general counselling that a good form master gives and which, incidentally, was envisaged in the county college scheme. The 'consultant', as Oxford called him, would have an index of school leavers, he would make himself known to them and to their parents and would have firsthand knowledge of the neighbourhood's facilities for adolescents. He would, of course, co-operate with employers and the Youth Employment Service but he would also hear of the youngster's job from the latter's own point of view. This he would relate to leisure-time needs and assist the boy or girl to make the necessary contacts. All three areas agreed firmly on one thing, viz. that the adolescent ought to have ready access to advice about youth groups and other opportunities for leisure. Whether the provider of this should be a voluntary worker or a paid official and by whom he should be employed is not a point for this Report to judge. It is obviously a matter that needs much consideration.

To sum up. The enquirers found that the whole question of recruiting was one of the weaker sides of the youth groups. Though the case for joining must be continually presented to the youngster and his own social world, the enquirers agreed that shock tactics are almost useless. Their findings on this point confirmed what the 1942 Registration Scheme indicated, that though barnstorming may, at a pinch, induce the youngster to join an organization he does not stay in it. The right unit has first to be brought to the notice of the right youngster and then the more socially inept he is, the more unobtrusive help he will need, perhaps for months, to fit himself into the new group. All of which emphasizes that it is all important to establish a friendly relationship with the new member. Nottingham, as has been said before, went a step further. It urged the point that the low-level youngster who has most need of the youth organization will seldom join until family pressure—public opinion among the adults of his own social world—is put on him. Before this can happen the artisan parent needs to be convinced of two things, first that even those of his family who are as old as their teens still require some help and direction with their pleasures; and secondly that the youth organization has real value and it is not just a place where the youngster goes to while away the time. The way to create a public opinion of this kind is, of course, for the unit to get on terms with the adult population of the local street. All told, therefore, the enquirers echoed what any leader knows, viz. that joining, 'wastage', and effective membership are far less matters of age grouping and activities than of a relationship between persons.

CONCLUSIONS RELATING TO THE SERVICE OF YOUTH

The above comment has dealt with matters which, by and large, the unit could control for itself. The London team, stepping somewhat outside the terms of reference, felt impelled to ask certain questions about the machinery of the Service of Youth. Had it fulfilled the high hopes entertained at its inception in 1939? That it provided valuable material benefits was not in dispute: but what might have been a new and exciting experiment in the co-ordination of voluntary and statutory work seemed to have developed along prosaic and unimaginative lines. At the local level it is the Youth Officer who must undertake this co-ordination, but, as everyone acknowledges, it is a difficult task to create a unity out of such widely differing parts. In particular the enquirers felt that a reconsideration of the function of the Youth Officer was overdue. In some cases it was evident that the area allotted to him was so large as to frustrate his very real desire to make close personal contact with individual units and their leaders. Then again, his status and work in the Local Government set-up seemed to be anomalous. To take some examples. It appears to be the Youth Employment Officer and not the Youth Officer who gives advice to school leavers as to what units they should join. Or again, the School Care Committee is not necessarily in touch with the Youth Officer, who could surely help it in the placing of difficult boys and girls. Nor is the relationship between the Head of a Recreational Evening Institute and the Youth Officer clearly defined. The former provides the instructors for the units in the latter's area but whether the two officials work in co-operation seems to depend on personal factors.

The enquirers' own contacts with boys and girls forced them to the conclusion that it was of paramount importance for the Youth Officer to know at first-hand the aims and pursuits of the young people of his area. They questioned whether machinery, however efficient, could reach the root causes of problems connected with the Youth Service unless it was associated with a first-hand knowledge of the local and current generation of boys and girls. One matter at least was incontestable, namely that someone should be giving personal guidance to the youngster in his choice of youth unit and other leisure time activities.

The London enquirers ventured to suggest that this exacting task should fall upon the Youth Officer. As an official he would have access to information, for example, from the Health and Probation Services; and as a youth worker he would command the confidence of the local Churches, Settlements, Sports Clubs, firms, etc. In his former capacity he could visit schools regularly, whereas to-day it is doubtful if many headmasters are even aware of his name. The school population would be on terms with him; and when they were ready to leave it would be as an old friend that he advised them which of the local units they would probably like best. Moreover his day-to-day contacts with the youth groups would enable him to see the outcome of his advice. Work on such lines as these, with the accent on the Officer's first-hand knowledge of the adolescent population of a defined area, would provide that stable link between individuals that is so vital. At the same time it would put heart into the more struggling units—and the Youth Officers were the first to admit how many of these were no

K

more than struggling. Additional work cannot be laid on this already over-burdened individual; if it is, it will have to be undertaken at the expense of drama festivals, games leagues, borough youth weeks, and so on. It is a debatable point whether these latter activities, which at present form much of his work, are really so constructive as for him to provide a day-to-day service for the weaker units, and above all to try to recruit the more needy youngster into some organization. The point is that a variety of agents should be able to arrange conferences and galas and even holiday camps since they are largely a question of administration, whereas a very special kind of person is needed to see which youth unit can best help the individual boy or girl. The change in function would clearly be an experiment, but the interviewers were of the opinion that the urgency of the situation justified its trial.

Another weakness in the mechanics of the Youth Service, as observed in certain areas, was the lack of any clear-cut policy about setting up new units and encouraging those started locally. One of the scratch football teams may be quoted. A local man, a capable fellow, was the leading spirit of this team. He needed only a little guidance for him to turn it into a stable, self-run sports club. But it was no one's business to shepherd him. Nor, the interviewers reflected, would it be anyone's business to take action about the petition for a gymnasium that sixty-one of the Northbury boys signed when they heard that an Enquiry into young people's leisure was being held. Another example of frustrated enterprise was that of the caretaker of a block of flats. He founded a children's group in a room above a public house. This flourished so sturdily that it outgrew the pub. No premises were available so he considered the possibility of erecting a hut on a bombed site and came to the conclusion that he could raise £300 and get the building erected with voluntary labour. He proceeded energetically until he was informed that main drainage, etc. would have to be installed, and that the cost would be nearly £2,000. Although these building requirements were probably sound, it was hopeless to attempt to raise such a sum in that district. So, as must often happen, a promising effort fizzled out because of material problems that no voluntary organization, with its inadequate resources, could hope to overcome. Questions of premises and finance are so frequently a deterrent to youth work that the London interviewers suggested there might be a case for treating the Central London boroughs as special areas, entitled to financial consideration and to some relaxation of the building embargoes. A more glaring example of lack of action arose over the question of a new unit for girls in a district which was very short of facilities. The Borough Youth Committee would not accept direct responsibility nor, because of lack of staff, could the local girls' organization undertake it. A Church, or some other local body, would probably have sponsored the project if a certain amount of financial help from the London County Council had been forthcoming. But no unit is eligible for grant-aid from this source until it has been in existence for six months. The result was that nothing was done, even though responsible opinion was unanimous that the organization in question was urgently needed. Doubtless all those who might have taken the initiative had excellent reasons why they did not do so in this particular case. The real disgrace was that, with an official Service of Youth in existence, a situation of this kind should have arisen. Nor was it an exception.

CONCLUSIONS—A SUMMING UP

The enquirers were commissioned to investigate one point only, why more of the nine hundred and thirty-nine boys and girls in the areas selected did not belong to any youth organization. At the same time they could not avoid commenting on some of the adolescents' more personal characteristics, particularly as observed in the urban areas. The first comment was that many of the youngsters showed a great amount of restlessness. Certain ones were always on the go physically, and many more seemed quite unable to concentrate mentally, discarding one interest or one thought for another before they had begun to digest the original one. In addition to this was what the enquirers described as 'apathy'. This was very noticeable among the girls, and especially in those who held low-level, routine jobs. According to what teachers remembered of them, most of these same girls had been reasonably alert as children. Whatever their I.Q.s, they had displayed a normal range of out-of-school interests, and had had their own modest skills. When they started work, however, they abandoned almost all their former hobbies, and their leisure became very desultory. This is not to say that they were openly unhappy. It was just that their mental life appeared to freeze up. The change may have been no more than a phase of adolescence, a kind of lying fallow before the responsibilities of maturity were assumed. But if so, why was it less apparent in the Grammar School children, and in those who held the better type of job? Or did the trouble perhaps correspond with a suggestion brought forward by other observers that, whereas boys tend to kick against an unsatisfactory post-school life by hostility and rowdiness, girls make their protest by withdrawing from life. There is a third possibility. Were the girls quicker than the boys to observe and reflect the view of so many of the adults of their own world that education should be directed at earning a living and that non-vocational skills are childish or unprofitable affairs, too frivolous for the serious interest of anyone who is practically grown-up. The whole problem of apathy, as evinced by the adolescent working class girl, and to a lesser, but still noticeable extent by the adolescent boy, was one of the perennial troubles of the youth organizations encountered. The enquirers thought that the Youth Service might be wise to enlist more help about it from the psychologists.

A somewhat less obscure matter which disturbed the interviewers was that so many of the boys and girls seemed to make such poor use of their leisure—their Saturdays and Sundays, and, for the school-goers, their long weeks of holiday. According to the schedules, more than a third of the Northbury adolescents spent their free time in a very stereotyped way, and only a tiny fraction had the initiative to strike out on a road of their own. To quote the London Report, 'A few programmes were indicative of time well spent but many showed the aimless activity of those who had little purpose. The lives of these young people were so anchorless and so few had an actual hobby that one wondered whether even the perfect club would interest them'. In Robin Wood, too, where the respectable old-established artisan environment was far less frustrating than that of Central London, the Report referred to 'the many who just milled around in the well-worn way'. The distressing part was that these post-war youngsters had a far easier life than that of the young worker of the past. As children they had had better food and better health. The material standards of their homes had risen. Their jobs were done in much improved conditions. By and large they had opportunity, money, and time for the stimulating leisure that most of them had quite enough brains to profit by. Every one of the Londoners, for example, could have got hold of books on hobbies from their public libraries. In Robin Wood they could have sampled such pleasures of the town as the theatre, as easily and cheaply as the pictures; and they could have joined innumerable societies for dramatics. That enterprise of this kind was unusual was reflected in the excitement the Nottingham interviewers experienced when they did meet a youngster who got pleasure from the kind of recreations that are normal to the average adolescent who attends a go-ahead Grammar School. Some were adventurous, of course, and shone like candles in a dull rather than a naughty world; but on the whole they made a poor, if innocuous, use of this new and ample leisure.

Occasionally, according to people more in the know than the interviewers, their leisure was not entirely irreproachable although the nine hundred and thirty-nine boys and girls encountered were doubtless typical of the thousands of adolescents who never come before a juvenile court for the relatively few who do. It is, of course, the latter who steal the limelight, and by drawing attention to the misdeeds of the few, distract the adult eye from the law-abiding lives of the great majority of youngsters. At the same time the interviewers were constantly reminded of the difficulties and temptations which did beset certain of today's adolescents. If certain ones did seem to be heading for trouble it merely confirmed the suspicion of any conscientious observer as to how many of us are gaol birds—loose. From what the interviewers saw of the upbringing of the small children of certain homes, it was plain that some of the adolescents, as children, had had a most indifferent training. All their gratifications had been provided rather than earned, and provided as a nuisance remover rather than as a sign of affection. Their punishments, too, had been less the enforcement of a moral code than an expression of some adult's immediate sharp reaction to their troublesomeness. A much larger number, probably most of those whom the enquirers met, came from homes where the changes in social security were too recent to have affected the traditional anxieties about poverty and unemployment. Such homes laid a corresponding emphasis on the importance of material possessions. Indeed the narrowness of the world in which certain families moved, and their hostility to new ideas and to new habits of any kind, was striking. Anyone who looked below the surface of some of these youngsters' lives could only be astounded at what their own qualities, their parents' care and their school's training had achieved. The miracle was that so many had survived so well the hazards of growing up in such unpropitious environments.

All this, however, did not invalidate the belief of the enquirers that, solid and right-living youngsters as so many of them were, the quality of their leisure would never help them to get anywhere either as far as their careers went or in making for a full life in other directions. At this adolescent stage they should have been beginning to dig out the natural riches on which they could draw in later life. Neglecting this, were they not heading for a dim little life, burdened by the trivial for the majority, and a trouble-filled future for the odd one or two?

What can be done to mitigate some of these problems? In broad terms, and in so far as a remedy lies within the province of the existing Youth Service, the troubles themselves fall into three categories. They concern a more adequate supply of societies, firstly for the adolescents of the rural areas; secondly, for the girls in all three areas; and thirdly, for the children below adolescent age in the London area. To take the country dwellers. The four villages of the Oxfordshire Enquiry supported seven youth organizations. This sounds adequate enough; but these seven had to cater for the whole of the non-adult population in four separate places. In practice they did not really meet the varied needs of the hundred and sixty-seven adolescents interviewed. The Oxfordshire Report stressed the impracticability of one organization hoping to serve several villages, since most of the older boys and girls had to travel to their jobs anyhow. It also thought that it was unsatisfactory for those in their teens to depend entirely on adult societies for their recreation. 'Although it is obviously right for adolescents to join in with the activities of their community as a whole and to become members of adult organizations . . . they are not given a sufficiently important role and are much frustrated by this. Nor do parents and homes always know the best way to set about providing for leisure even if they have the facilities. In any case home cannot provide the experience of group membership that is so valuable to the adolescent.'

As regards provision for the girls, the enquirers in all three areas were strongly of the opinion that the whole subject of the recreation of girls, especially of those whose full-time education ends at fifteen, demands more attention. In particular there seems to be a need for more skilled interpretation of how the organized group can meet the girls' own half formulated ambitions. Oxfordshire suggested that the organizations which profess to cater for both sexes should examine more closely whether they really are meeting the requirements of girls who are almost grown-up. The London enquirers suggested more physical activities, outdoor and indoor, for girls of school leaving age and thought that they should be organized on fairly strict lines. The older girls probably required less rigid programmes and more variety in the set-up of the group. The London interviewers argued that the girl's so frequent ambition to be married before long might be the foundation of an organization that at least sounded purposeful in this respect, and not only to the girl but to her mother, her female relations and her boy friend. The Nottingham enquirers, for all

Robin Wood's generous supply of organizations, felt that, somehow, few of them catered effectively for the older girls. It pointed out that the social ill-ease of so many of these girls was not going to be dispelled by an appeal to join some organization on the grounds of enjoyment. The girl did not believe that she *would* enjoy herself in a crowd whom she did not rank as her friends. On the other hand, a good many of these same girls admitted that they would like to belong to something, or rather to some people, if only they weren't so shy. The Nottingham interviewers suggested that organizations might experiment with an appeal to join solely on the grounds of usefulness to other people, with specific reference to the nature of the good works to be undertaken and (to allow for adolescent variability) a statement of the period for which the girl's help was required. No attempt should be made to disguise the disinterested nature of the organization, though the field of work, again to meet adolescent characteristics, might well vary. It would not, as in the case of the Red Cross, be confined to physical needs. An appeal on some such humanitarian grounds might possibly evoke the kind of goodwill that foreign missions tapped among women of all ages and social classes in an earlier Church-going generation.

A third set of youngsters who seemed to be short of societies was the older London school-children. It was definitely the London child who was concerned here, for no serious shortage of organizations for children was observed in either Nottingham or Oxfordshire. On the whole, too, the contents of the programme of the children's societies was sound and, roughly, on the lines of that of an up-to-date school. The interviewers and a good many of the residents of Northbury and Camdington all thought that more constructive leisure-time habits ought to be encouraged among the local children, especially the older ones in Secondary Modern Schools. They pointed out that children in their teens now have nearly fourteen weeks of holiday; that they have the whole of Saturday and Sunday free; and that even on their five school days they have finished work by half-past four, have no home lessons, and go late to bed anyhow. Moreover in their 54-hour playing-week these older children, even from the careful homes, are mostly left to their own devices. In big towns they have neither the place nor the equipment which helps to compensate for an environment that is essentially unnatural to the growing child. The ones who come from the less careful homes receive astonishingly little training in 'play'. On nuisance grounds they are almost thrust out of the tiny flats and packed rooms for all but their food and their sleep. From what the interviewers themselves saw of the younger brothers and sisters of some of the adolescents, they had probably had to fill in pretty well all their day, from the time they were old enough to sit on a doorstep, in picking up what pleasures and occupations they could find in half-a-dozen streets and a few back yards. Relatively few of them as they grew older had any idea of doing anything constructive with their leisure. Except for their thirty hours a week in school they led an extremely undisciplined life, messing about bombed sites, cycling round a few streets, and spending three and four hour stretches in the cheaper cinemas. An odd errand or so (for which they probably got paid) was apparently almost their only directed activity except when in school. Some of the enquirers thought that the schools themselves might give more after-school help to their own pupils. Although it appeared to be the London County Council's wish that the schools should take more action in this field, it would not really have met Northbury's need because so many of the boys and girls lived too far away to come back again at night. It was also worth noting that, whatever the reason, the local residents who asked for additional leisure-time facilities for school children preferred the voluntary independent youth unit to a recreational group attached to a school.

The London enquirers thought a larger supply of societies for school children was desirable for another reason, that it would accustom them to the idea of belonging to an organization. Neither the Nottingham nor the Oxfordshire interviewers agreed with London on this point. As far as their own areas went, it was the usual thing for the adolescents to have belonged to one or other society as a child. This early membership, however, had not necessarily led to 'club-mindedness'; nor to their becoming steadfast members of an organization in their teens. Children's membership was different from that of the older boys and girls since it was often a directed affair, pressed on by an adult. Moreover these younger children were very imitative. If one of a trio joined the Brownies or the Cubs, so did the other two. On the whole, therefore, the Nottingham and Oxfordshire interviewers did not think that the problem of adolescent membership would be eased by an increase in children's organizations. It can be argued that perhaps the Youth Service ought to pay more attention to the decisive break between school and work about which the adolescent himself was so emphatic. Those who discarded their Cinema Club, Sunday School and Scouts, along with their white socks and short trousers, might be displaying a properly maturing outlook. Sharp breaks are not necessarily undesirable when growing up; and for some youngsters it may be sound, as far as their membership of societies goes, for them to prefer stepping stones with exciting gaps to a parapeted bridge. The real point is that although the youth organization exists largely to help the youngster to move readily from school to job, and from childhood to adult life, it ought nevertheless to pay attention to his proper preoccupation with growth. Maybe all that the organization needs to do is to change its externals. But in the eyes of the youngster it is essential that all the time it should be smacking of his own more advanced stage. To him, if to no one else, it must keep on looking like a new coat, not just the old one with the hem let down.

The enquirers thought that there was not only a need for more societies, but that more experiments should be made in the provision of space and hobby equipment which the youngsters could use and pay for on an *ad hoc* basis. This would overcome the difficulty of their having to fit themselves into a group of people; it would meet their objection to being what they called 'bossed around'; and it might encourage them to set up more of their own self-run groups. That some of them were quite capable of doing this was shown by the scratch football teams, the cycle speedway tracks and the self-taught jazz bands that the interviewers came across. If it is objected that this kind of provision panders to the cranks and misfits, that it does not encourage the self-discipline that membership of any formal group entails, and that its standards will be low, the answer, as the enquirers found it, is that the existing societies do not touch two-thirds of the adolescent population anyhow. Moreover, the environment in which so many of the boys and girls live and the nature of some of their jobs is very frustrating. Then, too, they lack direction about the use of leisure since the adults they know have mostly had little experience of it themselves. In Central London, at the heart of the Great Wen, the crowded gardenless houses and the sterile streets deny most of the equipment which is necessary for constructive leisure in the widest sense of the word. As this Report must stress, the one positive idea that was most common among the adolescents of all the areas was to have more facilities for physical activities. This did not mean more football and cricket clubs, but more playing space for scratch games, more speedway tracks, more indoor and outdoor roller skating rinks and so on. Elaborate long-term provision was not the point. If more of the London bombed sites (which will have to be built on eventually) were roughly fenced and lighted this would ease the situation for at least one generation of adolescents. Direct cheap-rate buses to playing fields would be another useful experiment. Even in Nottingham the interviewers felt that there was a strong case for supporting the local plea that more of the level parts of the common land of the Hill should be freed instead of, as now, rented off to adult clubs. In the villages, too, there were frequent requests for more physical facilities, especially for swimming.

Another type of provision which it was thought would be valuable was a place—the workshop referred to on p. 126—where youngsters could use their hands and have access to equipment under reasonably favourable conditions. This would cater for both the maker and the repairer. It would furnish solid working surfaces, good lighting, certain basic tools and text books of the *How to Make It* variety. Materials in general demand would be on sale, and information would be supplied as to how the more unusual ones could be obtained. A kind of shop-keeper consultant would be in charge, but there would be no class teaching whatever. A charge for admission would be made, and as rigid a one as that of the cinema. Indeed, to the boys and girls, the whole affair would be on a strictly commercial basis. Nor would there be any suggestion that the workshop-user was being lured into joining a society. Another asset of such a place is that it would cater for the short and sharp approach which is typical of the adolescent. The weekly class does not do this. Next week is much too far ahead for the impatience of the neophyte, while a course that lasts a whole term is over-lengthy for the unstable tastes of so many adolescents. Indeed the workshop itself might perhaps be a peripatetic affair, set up in one area for just a few months, but during that time open every day in after-working hours and throughout the weekend.

A third provision that the interviewers thought desirable was that more help should be given about the reading of books, as distinct from magazines. The small paper shop that sells the latter by the hundred is a possible field for experiment. Could its interest in stocking inexpensive books be aroused? Should the help of the Public Library Service, so admirable in most cases, be enlisted even more whole heartedly? The gentle art of browsing that breeds reading takes time, and time is what the five-day week now gives, particularly to the adolescent. His week-end is not eaten up with the domestic chores as is so often the case with older people at work. On Sunday, for example, he may have nothing to do all day until the 5 o'clock picture queue begins. Would the Sunday opening of part of the Public Library (a reading room for fiction, for example) be too dreadful an innovation? Another potential promoter of book reading is, of course, the youth organization itself. Leaders, by the nature of their profession, are perhaps unlikely to be great readers themselves, nor, in most cases, is the youth group a suitable environment for sustained reading. This, however, is no reason for neglecting the subject quite so outrageously as do most units. People who challenge this statement might profitably do a little survey of the book shelves of the next dozen youth organizations they happen to visit.

CONCLUSIONS

Reference has already been made to some of the more common failings of the organizations encountered. Occasionally their physical appearance, cleanliness and tidiness, was neglected. Certain of the units paid scant attention to tools for creative hobbies even if they had fairly adequate equipment for games. Others were plainly living a night-to-night existence as regards their programmes. Others again only paid lip service to the task of trying to rise above the second rate tastes of their clients. Many were extraordinarily blind to the tremendous opportunities that awaited them as regards the below-average youngster. The enquirers also heard a certain amount of adverse comment to the effect that the unit was nothing but a rough house; or that the members 'thought they were above the rest of us'; or that the group's so-called educational classes never did a stroke of real work—the kind of barbs which any recreational organization is liable to suffer.

More searching criticism concerned the youth organization as such. In general this comment was founded on the fear that it brings external direction into the one part of the day when the youngster is not already being controlled by parent or teacher or employer. Too much direction may sap his native vitality and resourcefulness. This was rather different from another point made which was that certain types of youth organizations were over-authoritarian and tried to instil military discipline into children. Comment on these lines mostly came from independently-minded adults who saw life at its raciest and most colourful in the street and who applauded the vigour and imagination of the street play of the younger children. Allied to this there was a suspicion in certain quarters that the youth organization tends to replace sturdy artisan values by the anaemic ones of the middle class. Finally there was the theory that adolescents ought to accept their responsibilities towards younger children, as well as be willing to learn from those older than themselves. In other words though the youngster himself may enjoy being segregated with his age mates, too much of this tends to confine him to an over-rarefied atmosphere.

The interviewers agreed that though such criticism was often shrewd, much of it was arm-chair speculation from adults who did not know in any detail how to-day's adolescents do, in fact, spend their time. As far as too authoritarian a régime goes, the extent of this depends, of course, on what type of organization the youngster joins. The point is, however, that he joins voluntarily; and if he finds the discipline too rigid nothing on earth will keep him there if he resembles those youngsters whom the interviewers met. In any case the great majority of to-day's organizations reflect modern educational policy in that they most definitely try to encourage self-discipline, and often make successful efforts to instil at least the rudiments of self-government. The street versus club controversy was more ticklish. The street life of the younger children, e.g. in Robin Wood, was undoubtedly robust. But the local street was too confined a world physically and mentally for those in their teens. They had outgrown the quiet little games that could be played comfortably on the pavement; they did not like to be seen racing about as Cops and Robbers; and neither street nor park gave them sufficiently undisturbed facilities for a decent game of football or cricket. The lusty, free-of-adult-control street life that the critics of youth organizations so applauded was, as far as those as old as adolescence were concerned, largely a case of can-kicking, bottle breaking, corner congregating, cinema queueing and bits of horse play between the sexes. Much of it was spent in the absorbing and necessary business of merely observing each other, and probably most of the activities were right enough upon occasion. But to fritter away five evenings and a couple of days in the week in this way is a poor introduction to the hard won adult life of more-leisure-for-all. Some of the youngsters admitted that so much free time bored them but that they didn't know why.

If this Report seems to have dwelt on the failings of the youth groups at the expense of their merits, it is only because their weaknesses, however apparently remote, in the long run always affected the problem of why the youngsters left the group. But for all this harping on the debit side of youth work, the enquirers were satisfied that the case for the youth organization, as exemplified in Central London, in Nottingham and in the Oxfordshire and Buckinghamshire villages, was more than justified.

It must be remembered, too, that the Enquiry dealt only with *adolescents*, those aged 14–17. It was thus precluded from commenting on the work done by the organizations with younger children. In the past many of the most effective units have been the junior ones, and the enquirers found plenty of evidence that this still holds good. The children's cheerful descriptions of what they were doing in their clubs and troops and companies was convincing proof of their value. Another point. The Enquiry was carried out at a date when, because of the aftermath of war, the difficulties of the organizations were very great. In at least one of the areas meagre resources had to cope with quite exceptional problems.

Nothing written here should be taken as implying any doubt as to the soundness—indeed the inherent greatness—of the underlying purpose of the youth organizations. It, and they, have stood the test of time in a remarkable way. Among the many independent associations founded by men of goodwill for the benefit of the younger generation, the youth organizations continue to hold one of the most honoured places. They have indeed become a feature of English life that attracts attention from many other countries. Rooted in local initiative, they have built up for themselves their various national headquarters which, from a long experience, can be trusted to provide guidance without dictation. It is for public opinion to promote appropriate action about the local units, and for the Government and local authorities to give the support of their prestige, knowledge and financial resources.

The most convincing reply to the charge that the youth organization is a redundant institution was that given by the boys and girls who were themselves members. Those adolescents who belonged to a society were definitely easier to come to terms with than the non-members. They were not only willing, but able to talk, and they generally had something worth saying. And were not those youngsters who were active members a shade more reliable, a shade more open-handed than the rest? Perhaps it was mere prejudice, but it held for enough of the boys and girls over a long enough time for the interviewers to be genuinely delighted whenever a loose-ender did turn him- or herself into a member.

Even the most inefficient youth organization is always something of a civilizing agent since it encourages the youngster to tackle, on a tiny scale, one of the major problems of to-day, man's communication with man. While the personal influence of the wise and friendly adult is very important to the adolescent (as this Report cannot over-stress) it is seldom a substitute for his happy relationship with other boys and girls. Indeed it is generally agreed to-day that youngsters as a rule do not attain a balanced development without this.* The youth organization does another thing. It is opening the eyes of these near-adults to the fact that the improved status of the artisan world involves them in wider responsibilities than the traditional allegiances to the family and the immediate neighbours. It is harrying the youngsters' thoughts (and the verb is not too strong) into fresh fields. It is stimulating them to want to create as well as spectate. Compared with adult societies the youngsters' groups are enthusiastic, unhidebound and refreshingly free from bickerings. The members' youthfulness and the leaders' idealism make their joint venture, however outwardly rumbustious, an innocent world and a hopeful one—fertile soil in which to cultivate the good life. Perhaps the most infallible test of all is that they provide so much sheer happiness.

The more significant weaknesses observed in certain of the units were probably related to the fact that the function of the youth organization appears to be changing. It is, for example, difficult for a unit to have precision in its aims when it is uncertain whether it is primarily an institution where further education can be piped on, so to speak; or whether it is one whose most important business is to help its members to participate in an experiment in group relations. Is the organization a device for policing the

* *Boys' Clubs and their Social Patterns.* E. F. Piercy. British Journal of Delinquency. Jan. 1952.

child out of mischief or one for speeding him more quickly into the adult world? A more searching alternative that faced a good many leaders and committees was this. Should the unit for whom they were responsible be adapted to the 'average' normal adolescent, or ought they to think first of the under-privileged, the boy or girl who most needed help? The enquirers were in no position to give answers to fundamental issues of this kind but they did observe the following points. While ethical training has always been the concern of youth leaders, it could have been assumed in the past that the foundations of religious belief (which many regard as the essential basis of ethics) would have been laid by the Church or home. To-day, as has been stated earlier, a large proportion of the boys and girls in the Youth Service have no religious beliefs. The club with definite religious affiliations has a straightforward, if very difficult, task while the open club has an even more complex problem. If it ignores religion it ignores what, in the view of many, is an indispensable part of ethics and of the way of life of a civilized community. On the other hand if it attempts a religious programme it may either antagonize some of the denominations or it may so generalize the contents of its teaching that this lacks any dynamic force. Whichever line it takes it has always to contend with the apparent indifference of the majority of its members.

Secondly the battlefront of the youth organization has shifted. To-day it is less worried about material evils, those that beset the nineteenth-century young worker, than about the allegedly materialistic outlook of his twentieth-century counterpart. The more thoughtful Robin Wood boys, for example, appear to puzzle over mechanical and scientific problems, not the social, economic and moral ones that exercised the artisan adolescent reformer of fifty years ago.

Despite all this, the interviewers did not feel themselves justified in stating that the adolescents they met had an unduly materialistic outlook. Nor were the enquirers willing to affirm that to-day's youngsters are as weak-kneed, idle and improvident as some of their more critical neighbours aver. They wondered

L

whether the improvement in physical well-being has really been achieved at the expense of other things; or whether most of this comment is just the carping of crabbed age? On the other hand they did hold definite views as to the poor quality of so many of the youngsters' leisure in comparison with the opportunities that lay at their feet. But the interviewers criticized the youngsters far more on the grounds of wasting chances than of positive misbehaving. Something vital must be missing from their adolescence if so many of these physically healthy boys and girls never approach the exaltation that this stage of life is capable of producing. Too few ever indicate that they find the world is an exciting place and theirs to command—which is what creative leisure, at that age and at some ecstatic moments, should induce.

When the grandparents of these boys and girls were in their teens, a meagre cultural life for young artisans was the accepted thing, unfortunate but inevitable. If poor boys were not wicked boys they nevertheless could not hope for much more than a life of hard labour, with a brief physical respite at the end of the day. Little leisure and less money dictated pretty well everything they did. It was the exceptional working-class home in which self-education took place, the rather less exceptional one that in which a trade union or Church reminded people of their social obligations as well as helping them to cultivate many varieties of the fruit of the spirit. But all this was when the nineteenth-century pattern of English life still held good, and before it had undergone the immense changes of recent years. The economic stresses that used to affect every aspect of the life of the working-class youngster have been eased. The major physical needs of the boys and girls are met. They have leisure every day and in long stretches. They can raise enough money to realize most of their reasonable ambitions. It is true that the unskilled manual and low level clerical jobs in which so many of these youngsters are engaged may not be very satisfying. Their job may well be more frustrating to certain ones than they themselves realize. Nor must it be forgotten that the majority of these boys and girls in their teens are working alongside adults from eight in the morning

CONCLUSIONS

to five at night, from Monday to Friday, and for fifty weeks in the year—a very very different existence from that of the Grammar School youngster whose working day is entirely geared to adolescent needs. Apart from this, however—and the importance of a job that satisfies cannot be over-stressed—most of them have few major difficulties to face apart from family troubles and those accounted for by the vagaries of their own temperament. Moreover school has turned its skill on them with new techniques and an extra year in which to apply them. Some time-lag is inevitable between this remarkable raising of material standards and any parallel development in cultural life; but by this time the adolescent population ought surely to be showing the hopeful buds. And it is not; or fewer youngsters would be content to do so little with their leisure except to idle it away. That, however, is the picture as the interviewers saw it in Camdington, Robin Wood and the Oxfordshire and Buckinghamshire villages and as, presumably, it exists in the Camdingtons which are scattered throughout England.

Many of the problems the boys and girls presented were obviously beyond the competence of any Youth Service. The Oxfordshire enquirers emphasized that organizations developed to meet the need of the youngster in city slums may be unsuitable in rural communities which are only beginning to experience industrialization. In the country areas a wider interpretation of education may well be necessary, with more emphasis on making the facilities of the school and its staff available for the whole village, more training of the Grammar School youngsters to accept their local responsibilities, and more call on the educational resources of the local Churches. The Nottingham enquirers hesitated as to how far a youth organization is a suitable body to diagnose the new type of problems that the young worker of the Welfare State poses, especially in localities which cannot be dubbed as under-privileged. And the Central London interviewers, aware that so many adolescents are trammelled by a bad physical environment and, in certain cases, by the amoral code current among the adults of their home and street, stressed that a wider approach is required than any youth group can possibly devise or execute single-handed. Nor must it be forgotten that, even numerically, greater demand will be made on the Service when, in the late 1950s, the extra war-time births make the adolescent population larger than it is to-day.

There is another reason for advocating a more embracing approach. Beneath the outwardly uniform pattern of these youngsters' leisure lies a prodigious variety of personalities, tastes and abilities. This was apparent even during the brief contacts which the interviewers were able to make. A gamut of agencies is required to meet such diverse needs. The boys' and girls' acceptance of a leisure that is fundamentally dreary merely reflects, of course, the sub-standards that still persist among the majority of adults. That the youth organizations, for all their fine tradition, made only a slight impact on so many of these nine hundred and thirty-nine boys and girls, shows the weakness of the organizations far less than the strength of the inertia which they have challenged. Whatever the nature of the agent to be employed in the future, the enquirers were unanimous on one point, that the spark which first lights up the possibilities of leisure more often than not comes from the friendly concern of one older person for an individual boy or girl.

Appendix I

TERMS OF REFERENCE

King George's Jubilee Trust, the Sponsors of the Enquiry, was founded in 1935 as a national thank-offering on the Silver Jubilee of His Majesty King George V. At his express wish the fund was to be used for the welfare of young people. In 1949 the Trust set up a Standing Research and Advisory Committee to deal with the many requests it received to investigate problems connected with the welfare of young people and in particular as these affected the youth organizations.* One problem frequently referred to the Trust is the provision and training of youth leaders.† A second problem is connected with those who *don't* join, or who join and then leave an organization, viz. the 'unattached' youngster, and the 'wastage' of the group. Why do so many young people not join a group, and why, of those who do, should so large a number drop out?

The Trust decided to undertake an Enquiry into this subject and it appointed the Committee referred to on page 9. Its terms of reference were as follows:

"(*a*) To consider the membership of the youth organizations and to ascertain how this membership is distributed over the adolescent period; to analyse the duration in individual membership; to ascertain the causes of unsatisfactory leakage; and to recommend methods by which this might be reduced.

(*b*) To ascertain what proportion of the adolescent population is not attached to any youth organization; to analyse the composition of this proportion; to discover the reasons for its not being attracted to youth organizations and to make recommendations as to how young people who might benefit might be attracted either to existing organizations, or to new types of organizations."

So far as the value of the Enquiry's findings is concerned the following points should be made quite clear. It was confined to

* See note on next page.
† Since 1949 under review by P. Keunstler, Esq., Youth Research Fellow at the University of Bristol.

seven small areas, and its conclusions were not based on statistical material. No form of sampling, in the strict sense of the term, was attempted. Its aim was not to collect numerical data which could be statistically manipulated, but rather to gather the opinions first of adolescents themselves and secondly of adults who really knew these particular boys and girls and their background. It was therefore decided to study, as comprehensively as time and personnel allowed, the bulk of the adolescent population of certain small areas. These areas were selected as being representative of a variety of the social conditions found in this country. Though the findings of an Enquiry conducted on such lines cannot be extended in any rule-of-thumb way to the country at large, it is possible that they have some application to a much larger adolescent population than that of the areas here reported on.

NOTE

The majority of the youth organizations are members of the Standing Conference of Voluntary Youth Organizations. Its members are:—

MEMBERS

The Army Cadet Force Association.
The Boys' Brigade.
Boy Scouts Association.
British Red Cross Society (Youth and Junior Members).
Catholic Young Men's Society of Great Britain.
The Church Lads' Brigade.
Co-operative Youth Movement.
Girl Guides Association.
The Girls' Friendly Society and Townsend Members Fellowship.
The Girls' Guildry.
The Girls' Life Brigade.
The Grail.
The Methodist Association of Youth Clubs.
National Association of Boys' Clubs.
The National Association of Mixed Clubs and Girls' Clubs.
The National Association of Training Corps for Girls.
The National Federation of Young Farmers' Clubs.
St. John Ambulance Brigade Cadets.
The Salvation Army (Youth Organizations).
The Sea Cadet Corps.

APPENDIX

The Welsh League of Youth (Urdd Gobaith Cymru).
The Young Christian Workers.
The National Council of Young Men's Christian Associations.
Young Women's Christian Association of Great Britain.

ASSOCIATE MEMBERS

Christian Alliance of Women and Girls.
The Church Army (Youth Department).
Covenanter Union.

OBSERVER MEMBERS

Air Training Corps.
Association of Jewish Youth.
The British Council of Churches (Youth Department).
Central Council of Physical Recreation.
National Association of Local Education Authority Youth Service Officers.
The National Catholic Youth Association.
Toc H.
Toc H Women's Association.
World Assembly of Youth (British National Committee).
Youth Hostels Association (England and Wales).
The Church of England.
The Jewish Church.
The Roman Catholic Church.
The Ministry of Education.

Appendix II. Table 1. (See also diagram on next page.)

NUMBER INTERVIEWED: AGE AT INTERVIEW: AT SCHOOL OR AT WORK: EDUCATION

Area	(a) No. interviewed		(b) Age at interview		
LONDON					
Pilot Enquiry Northbury	128	*94*	14 years	26	*28*
			15 ,,	22	*14*
			16 ,,	37	*27*
			17 ,,	43	*25*
Main Enquiry—Camdington	261	*160*	13 years	20	*22*
			14 ,,	107	*58*
			15 ,,	46	*24*
			16 ,,	59	*37*
			17 ,,	29	*19*
NOTTINGHAM					
Pilot and Main Enquiry Robin Wood	64	*65*	14 years	6	*6*
			15 ,,	17	*13*
			16 ,,	15	*17*
			17 ,,	19	*19*
			18 ,,	7	*10*
OXFORDSHIRE AND BUCKS†					
Pilot Enquiry—Melbury	6	*5*	14 years	3	*4*
			15 ,,	—	—
			16 ,,	—	*1*
			17 ,,	3	—
Chadlicott	14	*10*	14 years	1	*1*
			15 ,,	6	*4*
			16 ,,	4	*3*
			17 ,,	3	*2*
Main Enquiry—Upper Hinton	38	*32*	14 years	11	*5*
			15 ,,	9	*14*
			16 ,,	8	*6*
			17 ,,	10	*6*
			Age unknown	—	*1*
Mersham	26	*36*	14 years	18	*17*
			15 ,,	6	*8*
			16 ,,	1	*5*
			17 ,,	1	*6*

(Note: In this and the following tables the figures for boys are in roman and those for girls in italics)

MEMBER OF A YOUTH ORGANIZATION AT TIME OF INTERVIEW

(c) At school or work		(d) Education—Past or present			(e) Member of a Youth Organization at time of interview*		
School 27	34	Sec. Mod. School	59	47	Age 13½–14 yrs.	12	
Work 101	60	Sec. Tech. School	24	30	15 years	12	
		Sec. Grammar School	24	3	16 ,,	15	
		Church School	12	14	17 ,,	28	
		Unclassified	9	—	Total	67	3
School 127	80	Sec. Mod. School	261	160	Age 13½–14 yrs.	68	
Work 134	80				15 years	15	
					16 ,,	20	
					17 ,,	8	
					Total	111	2
School 3	4	Sec. Mod. School	49	52	Age 14 years	2	
Work 61	61	Sec. Tech. School	4	2	15 ,,	9	
(at 1.2.51)		Sec. Grammar School	6	6	16 ,,	8	
		Special School	5	5	17 ,,	9	
					18 ,,	2	
					Total	30	2
School 3	4	Sec. Mod. School	6	4	Nil.		
Work 3	2	Sec. Grammar School	—	2			
School 9	7	Sec. Mod. School	10	6	Age 14 years	1	2
Work 5	3	Sec. Grammar School	3	4	15 ,,	3	3
		Public School	1	—	16 ,,	—	2
					17 ,,	1	—
					Total	5	5
School 21	11	Sec. Mod. School	21	24	Age 14 years	5	3
Work 16	20	Sec. Tech. School	12	6	15 ,,	4	8
Unknown 1	2	Sec. Grammar School	4	2	16 ,,	4	2
		No information	1	—	17 ,,	6	2
					Total	19	15
School 22	28	Sec. Mod. School	22	27	Age 14 years	4	2
Work 4	8	Sec. Tech. School	3	2	15 ,,	4	—
		Sec. Grammar School	—	8	16 ,,	2	2
		No information	1	—	No information	3	—
					Total	13	2

*Nottingham figures. These refer to effective membership over a period (see p. 69).
†Oxfordshire figures. Certain of these were taken from the area report; others the compiler took from the schedules.

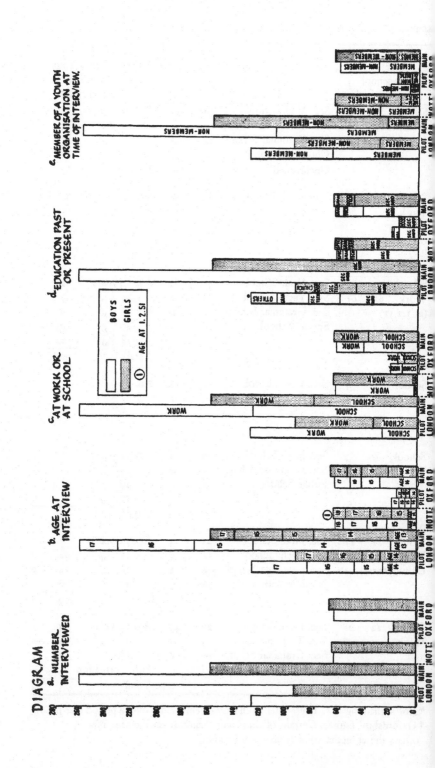

Table 2

NUMBERS BELONGING TO A YOUTH ORGANIZATION OR EVENING CLASS AT TIME OF INTERVIEW (LONDON AND NOTTINGHAM)

LONDON*

Northbury—

	Age 13½–15		15		16		17		TOTAL	
	B	G	B	G	B	G	B	G	B	G
Pre-Service	—	—	1	—	2	—	2	—	5	—
Scouts or Guides	3	2	1	2	—	2	1	—	5	4
Brigades	1	2	3	—	—	—	—	—	4	2
Clubs	8	6	7	6	12	5	16	7	43	24
Works Clubs	—	—	—	—	—	2	1	—	1	2
St. John Ambulance	—	—	—	—	1	—	3	—	4	—
Miscellaneous	—	—	—	—	—	—	5	—	5	—
Evening Classes	—	—	—	—	2	2	—	2	2	3
Recreational Evening Institutes	1	2	1	2	3	3	2	2	7	7
TOTAL	13	10	13	8†	20	12	30	10	76	40

Camdington—

	Age 13½–15		15		16		17		TOTAL	
	B	G	B	G	B	G	B	G	B	G
Pre-Service	16	—	3	—	3	—	1	—	23	—
Scouts or Guides	5	2	1	—	—	—	—	—	6	2
Brigades	2	4	1	—	—	—	—	—	3	4
Clubs	40	4	10	2	16	5	6	3	72	14
Works Clubs	—	—	—	2	1	—	1	2	2	3
St. John Ambulance	3	—	—	—	—	—	—	—	3	—
Miscellaneous	2	2	—	—	—	—	—	—	2	2
Evening Classes	—	8	1	—	3	3	—	2	4	13
Recreational Evening Institutes	6	—	4	—	2	2	5	2	17	2
TOTAL	74	19	20	3	25	9	13	8	132	39

NOTTINGHAM‡

Robin Wood—

	Age 14		15		16		17		18		TOTAL	
	B	G	B	G	B	G	B	G	B	G	B	G
Pre-Service	—	—	—	—	1	—	1	—	2	—	4	—
Scouts or Guides	—	2	3	2	1	—	—	—	—	—	4	2
Brigades	—	—	—	—	—	—	—	—	—	—	—	—
Clubs	1	—	5	5	6	2	8	3	—	2	20	10
Works Clubs	—	—	—	—	—	—	—	—	—	—	—	—
St. John Ambulance	1	2	1	—	—	2	—	—	—	—	2	2
Evening Classes	1	—	—	2	1	2	2	2	1	2	5	6
TOTAL	3	2	9	7	9	4	11	5	3	2	35	20

(Note: In this and the following tables the figures for boys are in roman and those for girls in italics).

* Membership of more than one organization (e.g. of Club and Evening Class) not shown. Youth organization membership was recorded before that of evening class.
† Small numbers partly due to lack of Grammar School girls.
‡ Nottingham figures. Refer to effective membership over a period (see p. 69).

164 SOME YOUNG PEOPLE

Table 3

NUMBERS BELONGING TO A YOUTH ORGANIZATION OR EVENING CLASS AT TIME OF INTERVIEW (OXFORDSHIRE AND BUCKS)

OXFORDSHIRE AND BUCKS

Melbury—No local youth organizations.

Chadlicott—	Age 14		15		16		17		TOTAL	
Pre-Service	—	—	3	—	—	—	—	—	3	—
Guides	—	1	—	3	—	1	—	—	—	5
Brigades	1	—	—	—	—	—	1	—	2	—
TOTAL	1	1	3	3	—	1	1	—	5	5

Upper Hinton—	Age 14		15		16		17		TOTAL	
Sea Cadets	—	—	—	—	—	—	1	—	1	—
Youth Fellowship	—	—	—	—	—	—	2	—	2	—
Youth Clubs	5	3	4	6	4	2	3	2	16	13
Red Cross	—	—	—	1	—	—	—	—	—	1
Miscellaneous	—	—	—	1	—	—	—	—	—	1
TOTAL	5	3	4	8	4	2	6	2	19	15

Mersham—	Age 14		15		16		17		Age unknown		TOTAL	
Pre-Service	3	—	2	—	2	—	—	—	1	—	8	—
Scouts	—	—	2	—	—	—	—	—	—	—	2	—
Clubs	1	—	—	—	—	1	—	—	2	—	3	1
St. John Ambulance	—	1	—	—	—	—	—	—	—	—	—	1
TOTAL	4	1	4	—	2	1	—	—	3	—	13	2

Table 4a

MEMBERSHIP OF YOUTH ORGANIZATIONS (NOTTINGHAM 1951)

The 36 units referred to are situated within 15 minutes' walk of the Enquiry area. Figures approximate and relate primarily to *adolescent* groups, e.g. do not include the membership of separate junior and senior sections.

APPENDIX

Table 4a (continued)

	Membership					Membership			
	Age −15		Age +15			Age −15		Age +15	
(Within 5–10 mins.)					*(Within 10–15 mins. continued)*				
Youth Fellowship	5	9	14	20	Church Youth Centre	15	25	10	25
Church Club	11	14	17	15	Co-operative Youth Club	35	4	20	—
Church Fellowship	4	2	6	14	Y.M.C.A. Boys' Club	60	—	75	—
Girls' Club	—	63	12	82	Y.W.C.A.	—	67	—	48
Girl Guides	—	30	—	5	Boys' Brigade	23	—	7	—
Army Cadet Force	10	—	8	—	St. John Amb. Brigade Cadets, Nursing Div.	—	20	—	10
St. John Ambulance Brigade Cadets	16	—	5	—	Boy Scouts	112	—	39	—
Boy Scouts	60	—	20	—	Boy Scouts	30	—	6	—
Boy Scouts	12	—	1	—	Boy Scouts	55	—	55	—
Girl Guides	—	15	—	2	Church Fellowship	16	17	5	11
Boy Scouts	32	—	6	—	Girl Guides	—	20	—	—
Girl Guides and Rangers	—	24	—	12	Girl Guides	—	35	—	15
					Girl Guides	—	22	—	2
(Within 10–15 mins.)					Church Club	14	26	10	8
Boys' Club	68	—	74	—	Boys' Club	35	—	40	—
Boys' Club	61	—	84	—	Girls' Club	—	30	—	6
Church Youth Circle	4	12	5	13	Church Club	—	—	60	10
Boy Scouts	20	—	1	—					
Girl Guides	—	24	—	4					
Church Club	15	26	5	4					
Church Fellowship	3	3	30	?	TOTAL MEMBERSHIP	716	488	615	306

Table 4b

ATTENDANCE AT 10 YOUTH ORGANIZATIONS (NOTTINGHAM. JAN. 25–31, 1951)

Figures relate to all those attending aged 14–17 (i.e. not only to those interviewed).

Organizations concerned: St. John Ambulance Brigade Cadet Division and Nursing Division; Army Cadet Force; 2 Girl Guide Companies; 2 Boy Scout Troops; 1 Boys' Club; 1 Girls' Club; 1 Church Youth Club.

Age	14 yrs.		15 yrs.		16 yrs.		17 yrs.	
Attendance	102	37	89	30	46	5	55	14

Table 5A
SEVEN DAYS' RECORD—EVENINGS ONLY (NOTTINGHAM)

	Number of evenings						Total
No. of boys 55				4 or	1 or		Number of
No. of girls 62	1	2	3	more	more	None	Evenings
Cinema	16 18	14 8	10 16	7 8	—	8 12	+102 114+
Evening Classes	3 —	4 3	— —	— —	—	48 59	11 6
At Home	16 20	13 13	7 11	4 6	—	15 12	+79 103+
Youth Organizations	5 2	5 3	5 —	2 —	—	38 57	38 8
Cycling, Sport & Dancing	—	—	—	—	23 28	32 34	—
Visiting	—	—	—	—	19 29	36 33	—
Strolling or Shopping	—	—	—	—	21 29	34 33	—
Other activities	—	—	—	—	25 26	30 36	—
No Information	—	—	—	—	11 4	—	—

Table 5B
CINEMA ATTENDANCE—AFTERNOONS AND EVENINGS (LONDON AND NOTTINGHAM)

LONDON—Northbury No. of visits per week	1	2	3	4 or more	No visit	Number of adolescents
Number of adolescents	52	23	15	7	55	152
NOTTINGHAM						
Age 14	1 1	1 1	1 2	— —	2 2	5 6
,, 15	4 5	3 2	2 3	2 1	4 2	15 13
,, 16	5 5	2 2	2 4	2 3	2 2	13 16
,, 17	3 5	8 1	4 4	2 3	— 5	17 18
,, 18	3 2	— 2	1 3	1 1	— 1	5 9
Number of adolescents	16 18	14 8	10 16	7 8	8 12	55 62

Table 5C
SAMPLE WAGES (NOTTINGHAM)

At Age	14	15	16	17	18
Girl—Machinist	—	37s. 6d.	—	80s. 0d.	—
Girl— ,,	—	37s. 6d.	—	50s. 0d.	—
Boy—Stock boy	—	43s. 0d.	52s. 0d.	64s. 0d.	—
Girl—Machinist	—	34s. 0d.	—	—	77s. & bonus
Boy—Apprentice	34s. 0d.	39s. 0d.	48s. 0d.	55s. 0d.	—
Girl—Clerical	28s. 0d.	35s. 0d.	40s. 0d.	53s. 0d.	63s. 0d.

Appendix III

ACKNOWLEDGMENTS

LONDON

Among the many people and institutions who responded with the utmost goodwill to requests for information and assistance were:—

Two London Boroughs	Councillors, Clergy and local residents.
London County Council	Divisional Office and Youth Organizers.
	Schools' Staff.
	Care Committees.
	Youth Employment Officers.
Youth Organizations	London Headquarters and local units.
University of London Extension Association	Westminster College of Commerce Group.

NOTTINGHAM

The Enquirers acknowledge with gratitude the ready help received from many sources including:—

University of Nottingham	Departments of Social Administration and of Education.
	Institute of Education.
Notts. County Council	Child Guidance Clinic.
	Combined Probation Committee.
City of Nottingham	Education Committee.
	Youth Committee.
	Child Guidance Centre.
	Schools' Staff.
Youth Organizations	Area Headquarters and local units.
Employers	

OXFORDSHIRE AND BUCKS

The Enquiry could only have been possible through the assistance and willing co-operation of many persons including:—

University of Oxford	Lecturers, Research Workers and Students in the Education and other Departments.

Oxfordshire and Bucks. Education Committees.
   County Councils Schools' Staff.
Youth Organizations Functioning in the area.
Employers

Those responsible for the Enquiry also record their gratitude to the boys and girls whose good sense and kind hearts made the work possible and pleasant.

They would also thank the many clerical helpers, and in particular Mrs. B. E. Towers.

THE END